THE POLITICAL
ECONOMY
OF THE
NEW LEFT

AN OUTSIDER'S
VIEW

ASSAR LINDBECK

Institute for International Economic Studies
University of Stockholm

Foreword by PAUL A. SAMUELSON
Massachusetts Institute of Technology

HARPER & ROW, PUBLISHERS
NEW YORK, EVANSTON, SAN FRANCISCO, LONDON

THE POLITICAL ECONOMY OF THE NEW LEFT—
AN OUTSIDER'S VIEW

Copyright © 1971 by ASSAR LINDBECK

Standard Book Number: 06-044018-X

Library of Congress Catalog Card Number: 75-178101

CONTENTS

PREFACE

MY PURPOSE in this short book is to try to interpret, understand, and scrutinize the economic ideas of the New Left. In particular, I shall attempt to discuss, in order, some of the more important questions on political economy taken up by this movement, *inter alia* to facilitate a dialogue between the New Left and academic economists. I shall emphasize some of the main social and economic problems raised by the New Left, rather than give a detailed account of "who said what." This means, in fact, that the book is an attempt to make a contribution to the field of "comparative economic systems." It should be emphasized that the "systematic" distinctions and classifications are mine rather than those of New Left literature.

The book was written against the background of my experience of political debates and the political literature circulated at various U.S. campuses during 1968–1969. The exposition is based on addresses to the Graduate Economics Students' Association at the Massachusetts Institute of Technology, Cambridge, Massachusetts; Columbia University, New York City; and the University of California, Berkeley, all given during the spring and summer of 1969. Somewhat shorter editions in Swedish and Danish were published in 1970.

I am grateful to William Baumol, Peter Bohm, Alf Carling, Frederick Clairmonte, and Stefan de Vylder for their comments on an earlier version of the book.

ASSAR LINDBECK

Institute for International Economic Studies,
University of Stockholm
April, 1971

FOREWORD

THE NEW LEFT is an important movement in the history of ideas. It is an important ideology in the political struggle for men's minds. It is the continuation of an important strand in the development of economics and the related social sciences, and represents a growing discontent on the part of students with what they are being taught in the universities.

Yet where can the open-minded reader go for a detailed discussion and evaluation of the basic tenets of the New Left? There of course are no shortages of tracts and treatises written by radical critics of the social order. And, if all you want are vituperative denunciations of any ideas newer than those of Herbert Spencer or Friedrich Hayek, there are plenty of books and Rotary speeches glorifying free enterprise and condemning atheistic communism. But no one, before Professor Lindbeck, has had the patience to collect together the various notions of the New Left, sift and analyze them, and finally to give an unsparing evaluation —involving both critique and acceptance—of their validity and limitations.

THE STRANGER AS JUDGE AND JURY

Thirty years ago, when the Carnegie Foundation sought to commission an objective study of America's racial problems, it turned to a Swedish economist, Gunnar Myrdal. Precisely because Myrdal came from a society that lacked our racial heterogeneity, he would be able, it was hoped, to arrive more nearly to objective truth. And so it turned out: *An American Dilemma* by Myrdal is not only one of the few classics in the social sciences, but, in addition, it alerted us and the world to the fact that we were an unconscionably divided house, only superficially in a state of equilibrium. The fundamental decisions by the Supreme Court, the Civil Rights movement, the struggle toward integration—all of these things which have become commonplaces were foreseen in the Myrdal study.

Once before it was from the pen of an outsider that America came to know itself. Precisely because de Tocqueville was a Frenchman, rather sympathetic to much in the ancien régime that had vanished with the French Revolution and rather unsympathetic with the nascent notions of American individualism, he was able to discern and extrapolate the characteristic features of a new society. If I wish my face to be drawn as it is, I must not go to my lover. Nor to my enemy. Only what is seen for the first time can be perceived in its uniqueness.

But not any stranger can pen the likeness of a revolutionary movement. Political economy must be grateful that Assar Lindbeck happened to be a visiting professor at Columbia University in the academic year 1968–1969. The right man was at the right place at the right time. To economists, Professor Lindbeck needs no introduction. Appointed at a comparatively early age to the prestigious chair in international economics at Stockholm University, Dr. Lindbeck is one of the young turks in Swedish economics. His grandsires, so to speak, were the great Swedish economists of the First World War period, Gustav Cassel and, above all, the incomparable Knut Wicksell. (Wicksell, who wrote one of his books from jail, never hesitated to speak out in good causes however unpopular: his views against marriage, against the monarchy, against religion, and against a Swedish standing army on the Russian borders kept him from a university post until the age of almost 50; his view that the worker would gain more in real wages from a non-Marxist evolution of the Welfare State lost him popularity in other circles, a fact which inhibited him from speaking his mind not at all.) Lindbeck's immediate teachers were of that vintage generation of Swedish economists: Myrdal, Bertil Ohlin, Bent Hansen, Erik Lindahl, Erik Lundberg, Ingvar Svennilson—but really the list is too long to enumerate.

Assar Lindbeck, though, is his own man. As a schoolboy he saw with his own eyes the flirtations with Hitler's super-race doctrines to which some Swedes succumbed in the days of the successful *blitzkrieg*. No ancient doctrine of Swedish neutrality has kept this soldier in the army of humanity from criticizing, criticizing bitterly, the United States policies in Vietnam. Just as in this country most economists have been associated with the critics of the ruling elite, the business elite—favoring the Democratic programs of the New Deal, Fair Deal, New Frontier, and Great Society, rather than the rugged individualism of Herbert Hoover and/or Barry Goldwater or the moderated versions of Eisenhower and Nixon—it has always been my impression when visiting Sweden that most of the economists there have been rather critical of their own Labor government. Economists, apparently, tend to be perverse! Lindbeck, however, is one of the economists who has been a defender of the general policy of the Social Democrats, though a "friendly (sympathetic) critic" of many details. It is germane to mention this because, if you are too far away from a social movement, you rarely have the interest or the competence to appraise it. Every day of his life, a Social Democrat is fighting through in his own mind the great issues of egalitarianism and efficiency with which the New Left is now engaged. No wonder then that when he visited Cambridge, New York, and Berkeley, Professor

Lindbeck kept his ears open to hear what was being said; and kept his mind open to evaluate the sounds heard. Moreover, a scholar trained in the European tradition can, thank heaven, be expected to know a good deal about the writings of Fourier and Owen, Proudhon and Kropotkin, Marx and Engels, Luxemburg and Lenin, Sorel and Gramsci, along with the more recent writings of Baran, Sweezy, Mandel, Mills, Cohn-Bendit, and Galbraith. Hanging up a picture of Che in your dormitory room is only the first step on the way to understanding the laws of motion of capitalistic development.

THE TEXT BEFORE US

During his sojourn in the United States, Professor Lindbeck was able to try out his first drafts of this book on audiences in Cambridge, New York, and Berkeley. It says something for the complacency of American economics that, prior to Lindbeck's lecture at MIT, many of our graduate students had thought of the New Left as having something to do with politics, not with honest-to-goodness economics.

The Swedish version of this book was published in paperback form under the title, *Den nya vänsterns politiska ekonomi*. So resonant was the response, that the book was soon translated into Danish; and a Finnish translation is now in the works. This present expanded American version is not a translation from the Swedish, but an English text prepared by Professor Lindbeck.

Who ought to read this book? I fear that those who need it most are least likely to crack its pages. Those who believe that Milton Friedman's modernization of Adam Smith is all one can know or needs to know about economic policy will hardly be tempted to spend an afternoon studying Lindbeck's evaluations of notions about manipulated consumer preferences or decentralized planning. On the other hand,

I hope that those on the New Left will not be put off by Lindbeck's occasional tart critiques. De Tocqueville's strictures on America were at first resented, particularly where his shafts went to the heart; but in the end we gained more from his work than did the supercilious Europeans.

When Lindbeck points out that often the New Left manages to be critical *both of the market and of the bureaucracy*, and that it is a sign of immaturity or of sentimentalism to think you can have it both ways, he is as little likely to be as popular with the groups he comments on as Margaret Mead would be if she called to the attention of the citizenry of New Guinea the oddity of their refusal to sleep with their cousin's cousin, or their insistence upon doing nothing but that.

An active member of the New Left will, then, not read the book in the expectation that it will convince him of the error of his ways. He will read it in order to give his views that severe self-testing which, as John Stuart Mill reminded us in connection with the necessity for free speech, is a necessary condition for conviction.

But most of all one would expect the readers of this book to be those who, like its author, have still an open mind on these momentous issues. You don't have to be an econometrician to tie in to this discussion. You don't even have to be a student of economics. No diagrams or equations interrupt this reasoned conversation. To be sure, the non-economist will not polish off this text in the time that he can read *Love Story*. But he will, I am sure, learn more from these hundred or so pages and will be given more to ponder over than if he spends the weekend grappling with the prolix sermons of Charles Reich's *The Greening of America*.

To the New Left most of the currently fashionable economic textbooks look pretty much alike. Any of them would benefit from being assigned alongside of the present work. Just because *Pride and Prejudice* is assigned in school doesn't make Jane Austen a dull writer; just because a paperback appears on a compulsory reading list doesn't make its subject matter boring or irrelevant. I may add that some unconventional economic textbooks, written by those proud to call themselves radical economists, are now on the way. This Lindbeck book will not lose in usefulness in being assigned as collateral reading along with such new textbooks.

THE NEW CONSCIOUSNESS

Good wine needs no glowing introduction. But I think it is appropriate for me to point out that Lindbeck's discussion has a relevance that goes far beyond the New Left itself. The ideas he is examining are not the esoteric views of a small sect of the SDS or of Village bohemians. Every single notion that is fervently held by those revolutionaries zealous to reform the bone and marrow of contemporary society are endemic in the minds of all of our population under 30.

It is laughable to think of John Kenneth Galbraith, although he is often cited by the New Left, as a revolutionary; and there is no shortage of critics from the Left who regard him as an echo of Thorstein Veblen and an apologist for the new industrial state his pen describes. Still, the ideas of Galbraith have an importance today that exceeds any influence Veblen had during his lifetime or since his death. For a better parallel you must turn to the role that R. H. Tawney played in converting the minds of educated Englishmen away from the Tory–Liberal dichotomy and toward a fundamental rejection of the acquisitive society. Alert Americans, before they have arrived in college as freshmen, have already read *The Affluent Society* and sampled *The New*

Industrial State. This helps explain why Ralph Nader is one of the most important men in America today. The fact that he is so is a reflection of a deep distrust of the business establishment and a similar suspicion of the government itself. This is not a passing mood which will evaporate once the Kent State killings are forgotten and a Vice President Agnew stops shooting off his mouth.

It is true that the campuses have been quieter in some years than in others. It is true that the ending of the Vietnam war will remove some of the deeper resentments of the younger generation. But to think that opinions have now reverted back to the hopeful days of John F. Kennedy is as naive as it used to be to think in the later 1930s that, once the economy had gotten its second wind following a malignant depression, the American mind had returned to the verities of Calvin Coolidge and Alfred Sloan.

Look at Lindbeck's contents page and purge your mind from any interest in the New Left as such. Concern about the quality of life is not the monopoly of a radical fringe. Or consider that tendency to reject both bureaucracy and the market as coordinator of resource allocation. Whatever its consistency, this strikes a resonant response all across the political spectrum. When Professor Lindbeck points out that the most elementary tools of supply and demand will correctly predict the inequities and inefficiencies to be expected from rent controls in the city, he will raise the hackles of every college student in the land—which is all the more reason why he should be read. When Lindbeck points out that Galbraith's model of quasi-absolute corporation monarchs, who tell us what to want and buy, lacks a determinative theory of how this one particular group of 200 giants happened to stake out claims to the areas they inhabit, the orthodox general-equilibrium theorist must hang his head in shame that he had not paid the

Galbraith system the compliment of taking it sufficiently seriously to have noted this lacuna in it; and, of course, no Marxian methodologist will be fobbed off with a model that simply has some group or agents having the ability to get what they *want* to get.

I could go on pointing out new insights that Lindbeck has put forth. And since no two people can be expected to give the same emphases in fields that are controversial and subtle, I daresay I could differ with some of the author's judgments—strictures against the critics that strike me as too strong, concessions to their arguments that strike me as gratuitous. Such tasks can be left to the future, to those polemicists who will spring up from both the Right and the Left to denounce the author for his findings.

Let me merely conclude by calling attention to Lindbeck's important discernment that one of the most notable things that is new about the New Left is its dominance by what may be called the university mentality—by youth. But before doing so, I think one disclaimer should be made. Professor Lindbeck is discussing the New Left and what I have called the "modern consciousness." He is not at all purporting to discuss that narrower movement which is called *radical economics*. Within American universities today the radical economists constitute an important trend. At Harvard, names like Samuel Bowles, Arthur MacEwan, Herbert Gentis, Thomas Weisskopf, and Stephen Marglin stand for something new under the sun. Elsewhere, at The New School for Social Research, American University, Stonybrook, Cornell, Stanford, the public universities of California, names such as Michael Hudson, Stephen Hymer, Edward Nell, Thomas Vietorisz, James Weaver, Michael Zweig, Douglas Dowd, John Gurley, James O'Connor, Robert Fitch, and Mary Oppenheimer represent to one familiar with the domestic scene in academia a serious research movement from which much will be heard in the future. The fact that other leading universities do not have members of the URPE on their mastheads does not mean that at those universities there is not among the students, both graduate and undergraduate, a growing interest in alternative economics to that of the standard textbooks. Since the time of Professor Lindbeck's visiting professorship in America, this movement has grown in numbers and importance. It was appropriate, however, for Professor Lindbeck to desist from judging a research effort that is just beginning; later, when the fruits of these studies begin to pile up, it will be inexcusable if the American economics profession does not give them the attention, and praise and critiques, that their quality and seriousness merit.

FROM THE JUNIOR COMMON ROOM

Who shall lead the revolution? Many answers have been given. The downtrodden worker himself. But not by himself, necessarily: with the help of the intellectual bourgeoisie. Or, in Lenin's reformulation, the professional agitator and revolutionist must be counted upon to shape the spontaneous consciousness of the downtrodden proletariat, sheltering them from the temptations of revisionist reform and cooling off the premature enthusiasms of disastrous utopianism.

Now Marcuses and Goodmans and Reichs have come forward to say to university youth: Who shall lead? It is *you* who shall lead. Upon reflection, the message is found to have merit in the ears of their listeners. Indeed, who is the most repressed by modern society? Who is most learned and least tainted with the rottenness of the older generation? The questions answer themselves.

I exaggerate, but I do not jest. The Marxian strategy of trying to understand the development of ideology and history out of the material conditions of production and class structure of society leads to fruitful hypotheses in this area. Youth, college youth, do not form a class in the conventional Marxian sense; but they do live under conditions peculiar to themselves, with a distinguishable economic base. And all *a priori* theories aside, one must accept the facts of experience: it was youth who formed the spearhead of the civil rights movement in the South. When white liberals were no longer welcome there, the action moved toward opposition, passive and active, to the Vietnam war. The fortress of the university itself came under siege in the name of "participatory democracy." The unmaking of a President, LBJ, was the fruit of work by young people in the New Hampshire campaign of Eugene McCarthy.

There is nothing new about this except in America. Abroad, the campus has always been the seedbed of social change. Korean and Indonesian governments have toppled when students shook the tree. The Japanese are great imitators of Western technology, but where radical activity on the part of students is concerned, and, for that matter, interest in Marxism on the part of the faculty, the Japanese have long been in the van. When the long-suffering students in Paris—now there *is* an exploited group—erupted in 1968, they very nearly brought down the de Gaulle government.

A class is formed as much by pressures from without as from within. Persecution of the Jews helps to maintain their group cohesion. By this test, students have come to form a distinct class. Students today elicit an enormous amount of hate, not merely from the hard-hat workers, but from the populace at large. When those over 30 meet for innocent merriment, their conversation about youth always involves the ominous pronoun "they." Over her third martini, the anxious dowager asks nervously: "Is it true that they smell?" What orgies of sexual pleasure are not imputed

to the integrated dormitory life? TV coverings of Wood-
stock festivals and Washington marches keep alive the
image of the bearded and long-haired barbarian within our
midst.

How can students be both against bureaucracy and
against the market, the objective stranger asks. The only
alternative is utopian self-sufficient kibbutzim. Yes, indeed
it is. Students are not out to make the universities like life;
they wish to make life like the university, the nearest thing
to the kibbutz one will ever know. Read *Walden* and you
will realize that Thoreau was able to lead the good life
there precisely because the rest of the world provided him
with the library books and the sustenance that could not be
grown on the shores of Walden Pond. Read Fred Skinner's
Walden Two, and try to draw up the balance sheet and
income statement of his utopian colony. I defy you to show
that it can continue to exist as a viable economic entity
without monthly allowance checks from parents outside
the community.* If simple living and intelligent goodwill
could solve the economic problem, poverty in East Pakistan
or Haiti would soon be a thing of the past. So it is within

---

*Since writing these lines, I have come across a most delicious
illustration of the rentier psychology that underwrites—oh happy
word—the Ivy League mind. Dwight Macdonald, that doughty graduate from the Trotskyist ranks, was asked at Yale what he thought
of Galbraith's complaint that Reich's Consciousness III was uncon-
scious of its own economic base.

Macdonald: . . . I think Galbraith's reaction ["Who's going to mind
the store?"] is philistine. It reminds me of people who criticize
anarchism by saying, "But who's going to collect the garbage?"
Incidentally, Fourier had a very interesting solution to the garbage
problem in his utopia. His idea was to have it collected by *les
petites hordes*—children love to play with dirt, so let them enjoy
themselves in this way. . . .

Marie Antoinette is alive and well, living in Mayor Lindsay's New
York!

the university. The commissary provides the bare minimum of nutrition. (That's all it provides!) Clothing is no item of expense in an era of bluejeans and bell bottoms. Where there is a sense of community and sharing, housing space becomes no problem at all.

But, you will object, many students still work their way through school, in whole or in part. True, but the number is way down: the night school is one of the casualties of the modern age. Even a state university must look beyond its own student body for switchboard operators and maintenance workers. And the places in which the students by and large must depend on themselves for subsistence, by contrast with the elite universities of the Ivy League, serve to reinforce the point being made. I have been struck when lecturing at commuter schools, such as Suffolk University in Boston or the Chicago campus of the University of Illinois or vocationally minded places like the University of Cincinnati and the Rutgers Graduate School of Business, that I am in a different world from my usual milieu of MIT, Harvard, or Yale. Indeed, the University of Illinois at Urbana differs less from Princeton than it does from the Chicago campus. To appreciate the difference you must talk with the recruiters sent out each spring by corporations to interview prospective graduates for possible jobs as junior executives. One of the questions that businessmen often put to an academic teacher is the wistful query: "Why are we in business so disliked? What can we do to change our image?"

For my thesis it is not necessary that more than 10 to 20 percent of the student population undergo a change in consciousness. Most of the world never changes but continues in the ways of their parents. So it was throughout the period of the opening up of Japan to the outer world. So it was in Czarist Russia, through the 1905 revolution and right up to the 1917 transformation: reading the novels of Russian life and the letters of political exiles gives a completely biased picture of what the bulk of the population is thinking and doing; but it gives you a useful picture of what the pace-setters of ideology and opinion are thinking about the future.

A reader of Lindbeck will be prepared to understand how important the movement connected with Ralph Nader has become. It is not primarily hippies or activists who mutter, "Right on," when Nader's legions castigate General Motors for contrived obsolescence through frequent model changes; if it were, General Motors would be much less worried. What many of the readers of *Time* magazine think today, the antitrust division of the government may come to think and act upon tomorrow. Therein lies the power of ideas.

To the reader about to sample the Lindbeck vintage, I say "skoal!"

PAUL A. SAMUELSON

MIT
June, 1971

THE POLITICAL
ECONOMY
OF THE
NEW LEFT
AN OUTSIDER'S
VIEW

INTRODUCTION

ONE OF THE SALIENT features of the New Left is its intellectual and political heterogeneity. This also holds for its economics. Consequently, it is rather improper to refer to *the* economics of *the* New Left; this movement has no well-defined and unified economic policy program. All that an outsider like myself can do is simply to draw attention to some of the economic ideas often expressed by people involved in, or influencing, the New Left movement, and to discuss some problems connected with these ideas.

The emphasis in this book will not be on the "grand visions," found in much of the New Left literature, of the historical development of capitalist societies. Rather, I have concentrated on the various problems in these societies that are stressed in New Left writings and on New Left suggestions about how these deficiencies can be removed by the creation of a "different" economic system. Most likely, many individuals of the New Left will not identify themselves with *all* of the ideas characterized here as typical of the movement.

Because of this heterogeneity, it is not easy to pinpoint the leading New Left economists. For instance, most writers in the innumerable New Left campus papers and pamphlets —a main source of information and inspiration for this book—do not yet reveal a strong and independent intellectual profile. Among leading European New Left economists, or maybe rather inspirers of the New Left movement, however, must be included men such as André Gorz in France and Ernest Mandel in Belgium, as well as such regular contributors to *The New Left Review* as Louis

Althusser, Perry Anderson, and Henri Lefebvre. It is even more difficult to say who the leading New Left economists in the United States are. However, it is obvious that "old Left" Marxists such as Paul Sweezy and the late Paul Baran, as well as a number of other contributors to *Monthly Review* and other Marxist and socialist magazines, have played an important role in providing a body of doctrine for the New Left movement. There are also a number of (mainly young) economists at American universities, who under the banner "radical economics" want to change the direction of economic research, partly to shed additional light on social and political problems raised by the New Left.[1]

The general attitudes of some members of the New Left movement have obviously also been influenced by Herbert Marcuse, though he has not said much about purely "economic" problems—except for his assertion that preferences for goods and services, as well as for political parties, are "manipulated" by the established power groups, therefore implying that existing individual preferences are not worth respecting. Among other ideas expressed by Marcuse and related to the economic philosophy of part of the New Left, is the notion that workers nowadays are largely integrated into the established socioeconomic structure and that the rapidly increasing numbers of students and intellectuals may therefore form a new revolutionary class of employees

[1]For a selection of New Left writings see the lists prepared by the Union for Radical Political Economies and the Young Socialist Alliance in the United States and by a great number of other socialist organizations not affiliated with political parties. A number of anthologies of New Left writings have also been published; for example, Mitchell Cohen and Dennis Hale, eds., *The New Student Left* (Boston: Beacon Press, 1966); Tariq Ali, ed., *The New Revolutionaries* (New York: William Morrow and Co., 1969). Another useful reference is David Mermelstein, ed., *Economics: Mainstream Readings and Radical Critiques* (New York: Random House, 1970).

because they are less closely connected to the owners and top management of large corporations than were the small staffs of white collar employees some decades ago. There is also the obvious influence of several of C. Wright Mills' notions—that a rather unified "power elite" runs contemporary society and that in the future intellectuals are going to play an increasingly important role in social transformation.

Among present-day sources of inspiration for the New Left, it is also necessary to include contemporary advocates of armed revolution, mainly in underdeveloped countries—men such as Mao Tse-tung, Ho Chi Minh, Fidel Castro, Régis Debray, Che Guevara, and Frantz Fanon.

In the perspective of the history of political and economic doctrines, the ideological heritage of the New Left has a much longer background. The sympathy for "direct," non-parliamentary action against prevailing institutions, so typical of much of the New Left movement, obviously harks back to the narchist and anarchosyndicalist tradition, including Bakunin's ideas about "propaganda by deed" and Prince Kropotkin's rather similar visions. A number of student leaders, such as Daniel Cohn-Bendit, have also looked for inspiration to Russian anarchists and other non-Leninist revolutionaries (for instance, Makhno), who were removed by Lenin at an early stage of the October Revolution from effective influence.

There is also the New Left's obvious general heritage from the "central" Marxist and communist tradition—in particular that of Marx, Lenin, and Trotsky. By Marxist and communist heritage I mean a number of well-known, mutually correlated ideas from traditional Marxist literature: that the "mode of production" (including both technology and the structure of ownership) determines the "division of labor," which is regarded as the main criterion for the division of society into economic and social classes and is thus the basis for "class conflict"; that class conflict determines the main course of history; that the owners of the means of production expropriate a considerable part of the "surplus value" of the working class; that values and institutions, in particular the state, adjust, like a "superstructure," to the interest of the property-owning class; that labor itself has been "degraded" to a commodity which is sold on the market, making "self-realization" through work impossible; that the system sooner or later will be overthrown by revolution because of the inherent contradictions within the system itself (such as the contradiction between degrading monotonous work and the individual's desire for self-realization, which produces "alienation" and dissatisfaction; or the contradiction between the increasing social character of production and the individual ownership of the means of production).

Characteristic of the special brands of Marxism found in much New Left literature is the emphasis on the critique of the division of labor and the frequent elaboration of the related concept of "alienation," both of which are ideas that are particularly characteristic of the writings of the young Marx and his Hegelian predecessors. It also seems that the concept of "class struggle" is broadened, in New Left writings, to refer to a general competition for power between various groups in a complex social structure—a competition in which the struggle of the division of income (the "surplus value") is only one aspect. In contrast to the "determinism" of traditional Marxism, the New Left does not regard as inevitable a revolution of the proletariat followed by the "dictatorship of the proletariat"; among the conceivable alternatives mentioned are a "bourgeoisie dictatorship" or other types of bourgeoisie domination, possibly combined with granting of minor "concessions" to workers in the form of consumption, leisure, and entertainment.

The New Left's preference for decentralization and its vision of a society built on producers' cooperatives with a nonhierarchical decision-making structure, can be traced back to such pre-Marxist socialists as François M. C. Fourier, Pierre Joseph Proudhon and Robert Owen.

Obviously, the ideas about "manipulation" of consumers and voters, with the inference that their "choices" should not necessarily be accepted, go back much further than Marcuse; those arguments are, in fact, rather similar to the classical (left wing and right wing) criticism of Western democracy. Arguments about manipulation are also somewhat related to Antonio Gramsci's notion of bourgeois "hegemony" in the formation of political and cultural opinions, though the notion of *deliberate* actions implied in the concept of "manipulation" was not central to Gramsci's ideology. The theory of "the manipulated consumer" is also consistent with John Kenneth Galbraith's ideas about the formation of consumer preferences by large corporations. In fact, many of the New Left's arguments against advanced capitalist societies are strikingly similar to those expressed in *The New Industrial State*, although Galbraith's admiration for the large corporation and his concrete proposals (or, rather, his lack of *far-reaching* proposals) are, of course, unacceptable to the New Left. Thus, the similarities between Galbraith and the New Left seem to lie in their assumptions rather than their conclusions. There is also a good deal of criticism of Marcuse and Galbraith in much of the New Left literature, particularly of their "non-Marxian" approach and their deemphasis of the role of worker movements in the future transformation of society. Nevertheless, it is sometimes useful, I believe, to use Marcuse and Galbraith as bench marks when analyzing New Left ideas. When "typical" New Left opinions are quoted in this book, they will often be picked from the works of the leading *inspirers* of the New Left, rather than from the works of (so far) rather unknown students and New Left campus leaders. This is the reason why there are many references to, and quotations from, revolutionary socialists of "older" generations— from Marx and Lenin to Baran, Sweezy, Gorz, Mandel, and others. Similar formulations are found in much of the campus literature, though sometimes in a less academic form.

By focusing here on the *economics* of the New Left, a small subset of New Left ideas is in fact separated out and scrutinized in isolation. Not only the general intellectual background of the New Left movement as just sketched, but also its historical origins and tactics—tactics such as those used in its demonstrations for civil rights in the United States, in its opposition to the Vietnam war, its demands for increased student influence at the universities, its awakening of young people to the poverty in underdeveloped countries—will largely be ignored.

Nevertheless, this concentration on one particular component of the program of the New Left, its economics, seems useful, if the discussion is to be substantive and not get bogged down in a welter of generalities.

The salient features of New Left economics are, of course, its critique of present-day capitalist societies, with the important role played by large corporations, and the vision of how the economy should be reorganized. A closely related though somewhat different point is its critique of economists and of economic theory, as it is usually taught at universities in most of the Western world. It is convenient to start with the New Left's position on this latter point, before entering on the main point of the book—an analysis of the New Left's critique of the structure and performance of capitalist societies.

PART ONE

THE NEW LEFT'S CRITIQUE OF "TRADITIONAL" ECONOMICS

OUR DISCUSSION of the New Left critique of economists and economic theory in this part will be mainly "descriptive." I shall also try, however, to indicate to what extent the criticisms are, in my opinion, warranted. I shall try to see to what extent the economics profession has covered the areas of research in which the New Left asks for more, better, and different studies. As will be seen in the later, more analytical part of this book, the New Left's critique of economists also provides useful background for our analysis of its criticisms of capitalism and its suggestions for the creation of a "different" economic system.

Basically, academic economists are criticized by New Left writers for studying the "wrong" problems. Even if the criticism usually is not very systematic, it would seem that the New Left has pointed out five major types of problems which conventional economists are said to have neglected. I shall take up each of these problems in turn in the following sections.

THE TRADITIONAL THEORY OF DISTRIBUTION

First, academic economists are said to have insufficiently studied problems of the *distribution of income, wealth, and economic power* in society. It may be tempting to answer that the concept of distribution has been at the center of economic theory at least since David Ricardo's work at the beginning of the last century. However, I think it should be admitted that, although economists have been interested in problems of distribution, their analysis has often been based on the breakdown of income and wealth into very large aggregates, such as overall profits and wages, whereas the more individual (personal) distribution within small subgroups has probably received less attention. Typically, when economic theory deals with individual behavior units—"microtheory"—the focus is usually on the "representative" household or the "representative" firm, in the Marshallian tradition, which, incidentally, makes perfect sense when microtheory is used basically as a building block for analysis of the economy as a whole, that is, for macrotheory.

It must also be pointed out that problems of the personal distribution of income were analyzed quite extensively in the older literature of economics—for instance, during the first two decades of this century—particularly in Pareto's writings and in connection with the theory and policy of taxation and public finance. As a general statement, however, I think it is safe to say that the development of the theory and analysis of distribution problems has been considerably weaker than the development in many other branches of economics *during the period since World War II*, when problems concerning economic stability, growth, and efficiency have received more attention.

It is probably also fair to say that "academic" economic theories of the distribution of income are still based on the marginal productivity analysis—and hence on demand–supply models—though somewhat modified by such institutional considerations as the influence of labor market organizations, monopolistic practices in commodity and labor markets, and income redistribution by government. This means, of course, that the distribution of income (before taxes and government transfers) is assumed to be determined mainly by the marginal products of the various factors of production and by the ownership of those factors

—labor, "human capital," physical capital, and financial assets—in society.

It is not clear if, and to what extent, the suggestions implied in the New Left's criticisms of current distribution analysis differ very much from this approach. It does seem, however, that the emphasis in New Left writings is more on institutional arrangements and on the role of notions of the "distribution of power" and the "class struggle" in explaining the distribution of income. Among New Left writers with a formal training in economic theory there also seems to be an interest in alternative macroeconomic theories of distribution associated with such critics of marginal-productivity theories as Joan Robinson and Nicholas Kaldor. Until such alternative approaches have been developed rigorously and subjected to serious empirical research, it is difficult to claim "superiority" for such models as compared to traditional academic theories of distribution. Often it seems that the New Left exposition of distribution problems is based on some version of a Marxian labor theory of value with the notion that labor is the only factor of production (or that all other factors can be "derived" from labor) and that a considerable part of the surplus value is expropriated by the capitalists.

In my opinion, a valid New Left criticism of the traditional theory of income distribution is its typically "static" nature. Economists have, in fact, generally not studied the "dynamic" socioeconomic processes very deeply over long periods of time during which the productivity of different individuals is *changed* (by schooling, by on-the-job training, as well as by the influence of the whole environment on the individual); they have also largely neglected the development of the distribution of capital over time (for instance, through the system of inheritance). However, it does seem that just these problems have in recent years been studied more and more by academic economists, such as Gary Becker and Jacob Mincer, to mention just two examples, rather than from the critical stance of the New Leftists.

TRADITIONAL EMPHASIS ON RESOURCE ALLOCATION WITH GIVEN TASTES

A second type of New Left criticism of conventional economics is that economists tend to utilize too partial an approach in their analysis of problems of the allocation of production factors among different production sectors, that is, to the problems of the *allocation of resources*. In particular, economists are criticized for taking household preferences mainly as given, thereby leaving investigation of the formation of such preferences to other disciplines, such as sociology, which has in fact meant that today very little is known about the formation of preferences that is useful for economic analysis. When looking at the research literature on the formation of preferences, including the effects of advertising and the influence of interpersonal relations on these preferences, it is quite obvious that the literature is basically weak in comparison with other areas in economics. It does, therefore, seem that this criticism is well grounded, though this area of research may prove a particularly difficult one, and it should not be forgotten that it was an economist—Thorstein Veblen—who first made an important point of the formation of preferences—the "Veblen effect."

In fact, it is not quite clear how effective research in this field can be carried out. Some New Left writers obviously regard theories about "bourgeoisie domination" and "manipulation" of institutions, values, and preferences as the natural approach to the study of the problem of the formation of preferences. This, of course, fits in quite well with the Marxist theory of the development of a "superstructure" of institutions serving the interests of capitalists and with, for instance, Gramsci's theory of bourgeoisie domination.

Most social scientists presumably want more flexible and "open-minded" studies of the extremely complex mechanisms by which values and preferences are formed and changed in present-day societies. The activities of large corporations, of dominant groups of property owners, of the military establishment, and the political leaders may, of course, be important subjects of such studies—together with studies of the role of labor-union leaders, minority groups, and various protest groups, including the New Left movement itself. As long as research in this difficult field is in its present "underdeveloped" state, speculations will presumably always fill the vacuum created by the lack of scientific knowledge; this means that both the "ultraliberal" notion of the basic autonomy of individual preferences and its opposite, the notion of the manipulated consumer, may well coexist for a long time to come.

THE QUALITY OF LIFE

A third criticism of economics, to some extent related to New Left views on the role of preferences, is that the profession has paid much too little attention to problems of the *quality of life*, compared to that paid to the quantity and composition of output of commodities and services. Part of the criticism is that in their analysis economists concentrate on the satisfaction of preferences for consumer goods, and possibly for leisure time, thus partly neglecting such problems as working conditions, the ways in which decisions are made, and the problem of the quality of the general environment, natural as well as man-made—basically, problems related to the "externalities" of production and consumption.

Sometimes this criticism, too, is given a Marxist flavor,

by tying it to Marxist notions of the "obsession" of capitalists with the accumulation of capital and the "unlimited" expansion of production, regardless of other values in society. Deterioration of the environment, alienation in work, and neglect of collective services are thus seen as unavoidable characteristics of a capitalist society; increased profits and GNP are said to be the dominating indexes of and incentives for capitalist "development."

In defense of economists on this point, it may be argued that economic theory has dealt quite extensively with problems of "external effects," such as pollution and city blight, extensively enough even to constitute a foundation for policy action, at least since the classical treatment of welfare economics by Pigou at the time of World War I. Thus, in this field traditional economists no doubt have an acceptable theory to explain environmental deterioration: the theory of "external" effects, which shows how a nonoptimal allocation of resources emerges when the productive activities of individual firms and the consumption of individual households influence the production process in other firms or the well-being of other households. There is also an interesting and rapidly growing literature in which various methods (like tax-subsidy programs) of dealing with externalities are analyzed.

There also exists a considerable literature in labor economics and social insurance—a literature in which relations between economic and social conditions are analyzed closely. I think it must be admitted, however, that there has been a tendency for the externalities to slip down to the footnotes, particularly in our textbooks, and that social conditions have hardly been at the center of the analysis in economic textbooks.

One reason for the neglect of the external effects of modern technology on our environment is probably that until recently we did not have much information about the enormous dimensions of these externalities. It is also quite likely that these conditions—in the form of air, water, and land pollution—have increased drastically during recent decades. Perhaps the environment is also a "luxury good," in the sense that people do not give high priority to the environment until their standard of living in terms of consumption goods has reached a rather substantial level. It does seem, however, that air, water, and land pollution now has reached such dimensions that countries with low standards of living probably also now have reason to be concerned about some of the external effects on the natural and man-made environment. In fact, this problem has ceased to be national and has become international in scope.

It is thus high time that a dynamic version of the Walrasian general-equilibrium system of economic analysis be related to the ecological equilibrium system of our natural environment, as well as to the man-made environmental system. Blame for the neglect of externality problems in practical policy in all countries should, of course, be laid not only at the door of economists. Politicians and the electorate are more to blame than economic theorists. After all, far-reaching suggestions for action against external effects on our environment have been constantly offered by natural and social scientists for at least a decade.

LARGE VERSUS SMALL CHANGES

A fourth criticism of traditional economics by the New Left is that the economists are obsessed with *marginal changes* within a given economic system—that they study the effects of small parameter shifts, susceptible to analysis by differential calculus, rather than discuss large, *qualitative changes* in the economic system. In other words, economists are criticized for confining their studies mainly to "local optima," in the neighborhood of the initial position, rather than asking whether there may be some superior "total optimum" position in a society organized quite differently from those we know. Occasionally, marginal analysis is even labeled "antirevolutionary."

This criticism is, of course, related to the assertion that the analysis of the allocation of resources utilizes too partial an approach, for instance, by not studying sufficiently the formation of preferences. Here, too, the criticism is given a Marxian touch by the New Left when they emphasize the need for the study of great historic processes and transformations of systems when their inherent "contradictions" become too strong.

Thus, economists are in fact criticized for neglect of the important but difficult fields of "comparative economic systems." To quote Marcuse: "In order to identify and define the possibilities of an optimal development, the critical theory must abstract from the actual organization and utilization of society's resources. . . ."[1]

I think that this type of criticism of the economists' choice of research topics makes perfectly good sense. The literature on comparative economic systems is not among the strongest in economics. However, there have unquestionably been important contributions to some areas of this field, particularly on a rather abstract theoretical level, sometimes using analytical techniques which make the field difficult for laymen to grasp. For instance, the vast literature on market systems and the differences between centralization and decentralization must be regarded as a significant achievement in the field of comparative economic systems.

[1] Herbert Marcuse, *One Dimensional Man* (Boston: Beacon Press, 1964), p. xi.

The same is true of the literature on different market forms, on laissez faire policy versus "Keynesian" policy, on the role of price flexibility, and so on.

THE ROLE OF POLITICAL CONSIDERATIONS

Finally, the New Left criticizes economists for having neglected problems of the *interaction between economic and political factors*. In particular, economists are said to have avoided problems of the distribution of power in the economy along with its implications for both domestic and foreign policies. In particular, economists are charged with having tended to suggest that there is some sort of "social balance" and "harmony" in society, thereby concealing such phenomena as the conflicts and power struggles of individuals, groups, and classes. For instance, the use of equilibrium models in economic analysis is criticized as a means of avoiding problems of conflicts and "disharmony." This criticism, too, is sometimes formulated in Marxist terms when the New Left evokes the notion of an "inevitable" class struggle and condemns the emergence of political institutions designed to maintain capitalist exploitation of workers and bourgeoisie domination, in order to conserve the basic power structure of society.

With respect to *domestic* policy, the criticism seems to be mainly that economists have not studied sufficiently enough the activities of economically and politically strong and well-organized classes and pressure groups. They have not examined the self-serving influence of these groups on legislation and public administration at the expense of underprivileged minority groups. I believe there is substance in this criticism. To some extent the lack of analysis of the behavior of interest groups may be a result of the tendency in economic theory to regard individual households and firms, rather than organized groups, as the crucial behavior units. There are, of course, a number of isolated studies of how, for instance, various types of economic regulation (of railways, oil production, radio and television, and so on) and tax legislation (loopholes) favor certain well-established and affluent groups in various countries. However, we still lack more comprehensive attempts at an overall view, partly because many important fields are still hardly penetrated by empirical analysis.

Where it concerns *foreign* policy, the criticism seems to be mainly that traditional economists, in contrast to Marxist economists, have not studied sufficiently how developed countries obtain economic, social, political, and cultural influence in other countries. They have not considered deeply enough the role of foreign investment, foreign aid, trade policies, military commitments, and general foreign-policy action (among which many individual actions may be largely beneficial to the "receiving" countries). In sum, economists have too much neglected the problem of foreign domination and imperialism.

There is, of course, an old economic theory of imperialism emanating from Marx and developed by such authors as Lenin, Rosa Luxemburg, and Rudolf Hilferding. It is built on the assumption that capitalist countries need military spending or a foreign "outlet," in the form of investment abroad, for excess domestic saving, in order to avoid mass unemployment. Certainly, this theory seems rather obsolete in view of the postwar economic experience, which has indicated that there is a permanent tendency for domestic saving to fall short of investment—with excess demand, low unemployment, and inflationary tendencies as results. This has been the general experience even in countries with very small military spending and insignificant foreign investment, such as Japan and West Germany. This seems to indicate that foreign investment, heavy military spending, and an aggressive foreign policy are not necessary for a high level of capacity utilization in capitalist countries.

On a theoretical level, the Marxist theory of imperialism can be said to have been made obsolete by the Keynesian revolution, which taught us how to maintain a high level of employment through deliberate "demand management," mainly by means of monetary and fiscal policy. Attempts at more realistic reformulations (for instance, by Harry Magdoff) have hardly removed, or even tried to remove, the basic weakness of the Marxian model of imperialism, though it has been suggested by Magdoff and others, that interest in a guaranteed supply of raw materials presumably might be a partial explanation for the foreign policies of such countries as the United States and the Soviet Union. However, these are general, common-sence considerations, which are not closely tied to the Marxist theory of imperialism—or to "ordinary" economic theory, for that matter. The same seems to hold for A. G. Frank's idea that powerful economic centers have a tendency to pull factors of production (particularly financial capital) from weak, peripheral areas, thus perpetuating or even increasing differences in economic power.

There is also a "new" theory of imperialism and militarism which seems somewhat more realistic than the old Marxist analysis—the theory of Pentagonism, as formulated by the former President of the Dominican Republic, Juan Bosch. According to Bosch, the main problem is not that capitalists in rich countries "exploit" workers in foreign countries, but rather that the "military-industrial complex" in certain rich countries, such as the United States, succeeds by means of propaganda and misleading information in allocating a substantial part of the domestic resources for military purposes. Thus, it is mainly the domestic population outside the military-industrial complex, rather than the foreigner, which is exploited, in the sense that it is denied private or public consumption opportunities which would otherwise be available. According to this theory, the military-industrial complex—consisting not only of military establishments and military-oriented industries but also of labor unions and residents in areas dependent on defense contracts—has an interest in a permanent cold war, possibly kept alive by some minor "hot" wars from time to time. Let this theory of imperialism be called "the Eisenhower-Bosch theory of the military-industrial complex." To some extent it probably conflicts with the orthodox Marxist theory of imperialism, for the latter implies that employment and production are kept up in the "home country" by imperialism in other countries and that workers in several imperialist countries must benefit from imperialist adventures.

Often however, the term "neocolonialism" is simply a label for the dominant role played by big business (owned by the rich countries) in less developed countries, applied without much regard for any underlying Marxist theory. Thus, big corporations are often criticized for activities in poor countries even when, in some respects, they behave against the interest of their home governments (as in tax evasion); they may also be criticized not for *exporting* capital to less developed countries but for *importing* capital from them (for example, from Latin American countries).

I think it is hard to deny that economists have had little to say about such problems, that is, about the relation between economic power and the political process. Thus, the New Left criticism of economists for this neglect, both on the domestic and the foreign scene, is probably well taken. However, in my opinion, these kinds of problems are best studied by means of more flexible and less dogmatic approaches than prevailing economic theories of imperialism offer. What is required, it seems to me, are concrete studies of the mechanisms by which various domestic pressure groups obtain privileges through economic and other types of legislation and of how foreign domination may sometimes occur through foreign investments, foreign aid, trade policies, military policies, and the like. Various economic interests—both private and public—as well as national strategic interests—for example, in the availability of raw materials—should of course enter into such studies.

Even if the Marxist *macroeconomic* explanation of imperialism as a means of finding a foreign outlet for excess saving is weak, there is, of course, often a *microeconomic* reason for individual firms to expand their markets in foreign countries: simply, to increase their profit. Obviously, such attempts have frequently been actively supported by governments in rich countries through political pressure or even military intervention. It is not difficult to find both historical and contemporary examples—the colonialism of the mercantilist period and the "classical" colonialism just before World War I—and imperialism of this type probably plays a part in today's big-power policies.

This microeconomic side of imperialism was assigned a considerable role in Hobson's relatively early writings on imperialism, as well as in Marxist theory, based on the assumption (incorrect, as it turned out) of a tendency to a falling profit rate in developed countries. On the other hand, it seems to be a mistake to believe that the business society generally considers foreign-policy confrontations advantageous to the business community. This is certainly suggested by the declines in stock exchange prices that usually accompany international political crises and the rises that usually follow rumors of peace.

EVALUATIVE COMMENTS

When we try to evaluate the New Left's criticism of economists as described here, condensed to five points and also probably "underdramatized," we may say that it is partly a charge that economists are economists only and not also at the same time sociologists, political scientists, psychologists, philosophers, and so on (or social reformers or even revolutionaries). In this sense, the criticism can be interpreted partly as a plea for more interdisciplinary research— a plea that probably makes sense. Sometimes it is combined with a methodological revolt against technical economics, including the use of mathematical and econometric methods. To some extent the criticism is also just a complaint that economic research is not more advanced than it is, which presumably will always be a safe point of view.

Basically, however, the New Left questions the priorities that economists as a group have assigned to different components of the workings of the economy in their collective choice of topics for research. I think it can be argued cogently that for a long time there has been a tendency among analytically talented people to produce small variations on formal models that have already been developed by others. The multitude of articles in recent decades on Harrod-Domar models, two-sector growth models, turnpike theorems, and so on, are, I believe, cases in point. Many young people seem to have been more inspired by technical-model problems of already published articles than by the more complex and "messy" problems in the world in which we live. The choice of topic has often been determined more by considerations of available analytical techniques than by substantive problems. Presumably, these tendencies reflect the milieu in which economics is taught, particularly in the United States.

In principle, priorities in the choices of topic are, of

course, a matter for subjective evaluation, but I think many people today would agree that "too little" of our best intellectual talent has gone into areas of great economic and social importance, particularly such "neglected" areas as the personal distribution of income, wealth, and economic power; the formation of preferences and the effects of advertising; the role of externalities; comparative economic systems; the interaction between economic and political factors; and so on. Obviously, we do not have to be adherents of the New Left to agree on this!

When trying to evaluate the New Left criticism of economists, it is also important to note that considerable parts of economic analysis do in fact deal with exactly those problems in which the New Left seems to be interested. One difficulty, however, is that the level of abstraction often is so high that the layman does not realize the "relevance" of the problems studied. This seems to hold, for example, for parts of the theory of allocation, the analysis of centralized versus decentralized systems, and the study of the market economy as a system of information and incentives. This means, then, that economists have not yet been very successful in the important pedagogical task of translating modern economic theory into a language understandable to the general public. In fact, it will probably always be difficult for the general public to grasp that basic research and the development of analytic methods are indispensable for the long-run development of social sciences.

I think it is also safe to say that in recent years there have been very strong tendencies to expand research just in those neglected areas emphasized by the New Left. We may mention the growing literature on the return to education (to help explain the distribution of income), the economics of discrimination, urban economics, the external effects on our environment from various kinds of pollution, and the like. There is also an expanding literature on comparative economic systems and on the relations between rich and poor countries. However, the Marxist branch of the New Left would presumably argue that conventional methods of analysis can never cope with these problems, and that a Marxist theory is necessary to highlight the relation between all these problems and the capitalist organization of society. The only way to convince anybody of the usefulness of various approaches to economic research is probably to let each person try the methods he believes in and then let the profession as a whole compare the results. This means that we have to wait some time to see if the new group of young economists trying to develop a new radical economics will in fact succeed in making an important contribution to economic research. If so, I would expect their contributions to be absorbed quite rapidly into the main body of scientific methods and knowledge of economics.

There are also some social scientists who have to some extent succeeded in integrating economic, social, and political factors in their studies. Two of the most obvious examples are Simon Kuznets and Gunnar Myrdal. Myrdal, from his study of the Negro problem in the United States to his analysis of Southeast Asia, has made the interaction among economic, social, and political factors the essence of his approach. Moreover, during the last decades, leading economists have clearly not confined their analyses to equilibrium positions of economic and social systems. Dynamic theory, stability analysis, and disequilibrium processes of various types constitute a very important branch of contemporary research. It is probably true, however, that textbooks still concentrate heavily on equilibrium analysis, presumably because it is easier both from analytical and pedagogical points of view.

It would appear, then, that the choice of research topics

by economists and thus the preferences revealed by the economic profession have already begun to shift in the direction demanded by New Left critics, among others. It would also seem, in my opinion, that the most important results achieved in these neglected areas have, so far, been obtained by economists using a rather traditional kit of analytical tools, though in many cases professional economists may have first been made aware of problems through the writings of nonprofessionals, such as Michael Harrington, or more literary economists, such as Galbraith.

Hence, it seems that the increased demand in recent years for new types of economic and social research has already begun to influence the supply of research. From this perspective, the New Left may be regarded as part of the "market mechanism" for economic and social research, contributing to changing preferences and helping to transmit information from the demand side to the supply side of research. Thus, the "wonders of the market system" appear to be sufficiently far-reaching to serve even the interests of the New Left. Maybe this is what Marcuse means when he talks about the remarkable capability of contemporary society to "contain . . . social change," "to reconcile the forces opposing the system," and to "integrate . . . opposites."[2]

It has often been claimed by New Left writers that there is a laissez faire or conservative bias in traditional economics. Sometimes it has also been said that the social sciences, in contrast to the natural sciences, must always build on political values. Objective research in social sciences is considered impossible in principle (although Marxists often argue that Marxism reveals the "objective laws of capitalism").

[2]Marcuse, p. xii.

It is probably true that most professional economists in noncommunist countries adhere to a nonsocialist political ideology and that this ideological preference is of course reflected in the recommendations for economic policy that many of them make from time to time, *not as economic scholars but as private citizens.* If advocacy of decentralization of economic decision-making and reliance on markets are regarded as the expression of liberalism or conservatism, it would in fact be true that most economists (not only in the West) are liberals or conservatives. It is probably also true that many years of studying economics tend to increase respect for decentralization and markets. I think this is a typical experience of most socialists who have studied economics for a long time. Of course, this does not necessarily mean that they will support liberal or conservative parties. They may equally well be social democrats or market socialists.

But to argue that all research in the social sciences *has to be* subjective and based on political values is obviously a misunderstanding and one that denies the important distinction between positive and normative economics. It is, of course, possible to study the effects on prices and quantities in the oil industry of a tax on gasoline, regardless of our feelings about the tax or about the oil industry, for that matter—an example of positive economics. Subjective evaluations do not have to be introduced until we want to decide whether such a tax is "good" or "bad" in comparison with other alternatives—an example of normative economics. The only subjective element in *positive* economics is, in principle, the choice of topic; in this respect the social sciences hardly differ from the natural sciences, however. The same type of subjectivism in choosing topics obviously is involved when a physicist chooses to study some topic on atoms or a zoologist decides to study the eyes of fishes.

On the other hand, what is special about the social sciences, as distinct from the natural sciences, is that the object of study (man and society) varies so much in space and time and that the problems involved in carrying out controlled experiments in the social sciences sometimes make it difficult to discriminate between alternative hypotheses. As is well known, this difficulty may leave room for subjective beliefs, which in turn may be based on economic interests or ideologies. This means that even theories based on personal beliefs, ideologies, or just wishful thinking sometimes may survive for long periods, particularly if they are grandiose, historic-philosophical visions not susceptible to empirical testing. Another consequence is that value-laden concepts with political implications are easily smuggled into scientific studies, consciously or unconsciously. However, recent advances in testing with the help of nonexperimental data have no doubt narrowed the scope for subjectivity in a number of cases. This means that the "death risk" for erroneous theories has increased considerably—although, it is true, the grandiose historic-philosophical visions have not been much affected.

PART TWO

THE NEW LEFT'S CRITIQUE OF THE PRESENT ECONOMY

We turn now to the more fundamental part of the political economy of the New Left—to its criticism of the present economic order, and its proposals for economic and social change. Three questions will be posed: First, what are the economic ideas and suggestions of the New Left? Second, do they make sense? And third, what problems are involved in these ideas and suggestions? The exposition may be regarded as an attempt to take a look at the New Left's ideas from the perspective of economic theory.

It seems appropriate to organize the analysis into six categories, each corresponding to a classical issue in economic analysis:

1. The choice between markets and formalized administrative processes ("bureaucracy") as a means of allocating resources
2. The choice between centralization and decentralization in the decision-making process
3. The choice among private, public, and collective ownership of the means of production
4. The extent to which we should rely on material incentives, such as profits and wage differentials
5. The choice between competition and cooperation (or collusion) among both firms and individuals
6. The meaning of "economic development"

It should be emphasized that the discussion in the following sections refers mainly to problems in rather highly developed countries, with a fairly complex industrial sector. It is the New Left's ideas about societies *of this kind* which will be discussed here. However, it is important to understand that much of the emotional and intellectual inspiration of New Left thought stems from their observation of the poverty in underdeveloped countries and from the belief that this poverty to a considerable extent is "caused" by the affluence of rich countries and by the activities of capitalist firms in underdeveloped countries—a belief that is quite difficult to prove or disprove.

MARKETS VERSUS FORMALIZED ADMINISTRATIVE PROCESSES ("BUREAUCRACY")

One characteristic feature of the New Left movement is that most of its adherents are strongly opposed to markets. In the literature of the New Left, a market system is denounced as primitive, inefficient, chaotic, antisocial, unfair, and basically immoral.

One problem with this position is that most of the New Left's writers in this field are also strongly opposed to bureaucracy, that is, to formalized hierarchical administrative procedures. For instance, the bureaucracy in the Soviet Union is often criticized in New Left literature. Ernest Mandel is quite representative of the New Left when he argues that "the existence of this huge mass of bureaucracy [in U.S.S.R.] both reduces the consumption fund of the producers and also diverts a large share of the social surplus into unproductive consumption. . . . The arbitrariness and tyranny of the bureaucracy weighs more and more unbearably upon the mass of workers."[1] It may be possible to make a strong case against either markets or administrative systems, but if we are against *both* we are in trouble;

---

[1] Ernest Mandel, *Marxist Economic Theory*, 2 vols. (New York: Monthly Review Press, 1968), 2:598.

there is hardly a third method for allocating resources and coordinating economic decisions, if we eliminate physical force. Both markets and administrative procedures may, of course, take many different forms: Markets may be more or less competitive and administrative procedures more or less centralized, with some decision-making by vote, and so on. *Thus, the more strongly we are against bureaucracy, the more we should be in favor of markets.*

Obviously, many adherents of the New Left do not feel that they are in trouble when they are against both markets and bureaucracy. And a few certainly have avoided the dilemma either by choosing markets (as, for instance, Murray Rothbard in the United States) or by choosing administrative central planning (such as more traditional adherents of the Soviet model). However, I think it is fair to say that most followers of the New Left have never faced up to the fact that we must have *some* mechanism for (1) obtaining *information* about preferences; (2) *allocating* resources to different sectors in accordance with these preferences; (3) deciding which *production techniques* to use; (4) creating *incentives* to economize in the use of resources, to invest, and to develop new technologies; and finally, (5) *coordinating* the decisions of millions of individual firms and households to make them consistent, so that each industry produces just so much and in exactly those quantities that are desired not only by households but also by firms producing millions of other commodities.

In an economy without markets or with only minimal markets, an enormous amount of detailed information is required by the central planners. Information is needed on both the production possibilities for all the different products (the marginal rates of transformation between any pair of products) and the tastes, that is, the preference functions, of consumers (marginal rates of substitution).

On the basis of such information, a hypothetical super-computer could in theory work out a program for an optimal allocation of resources. If, on the other hand, the authorities themselves decide on the desired "basket" of final output (without seeking to know and cater to "subjective" consumer preferences), information would of course have to be collected *only* about production processes. An optimal allocation of resources could then theoretically be worked out, for instance with the help of an "activity model" and a supercomputer—with "shadow-prices" for factors of production as a by-product of the solution.

Actually, both alternatives have to be regarded as formidable tasks, not only because of the limited capacity of existing and conceivable computers but also and above all because of the difficulties involved in collecting and coordinating in one place up-to-date information about alternative production processes for millions of different commodities. These difficulties will have to be faced whether queues, ration cards, or equilibrium markets are used to *distribute* the total basket of centrally determined consumer goods among households. Because of the inadequate information on preferences and production costs, as well as lack of incentives, we should expect nonoptimal factor proportions, nonoptimal holdings of inventories, absence of efficient investment criteria, and consequent misallocation of capital stock, as well as a poor adjustment of the quality of products and services to the wishes of buyers. This expectation seems quite consistent with empirical evidence from the Soviet Union and Eastern Europe. In fact, it has been difficult in those countries even to obtain reasonable *consistency* in input-output relations, and it seems that the striving after such consistency has often completely overshadowed attempts to achieve efficient and approximately optimal allocation of resources, including the choice of product quality.[2]

Where strongly centralized economies seem to have been most successful is in the mobilization of underutilized resources and in keeping down the share of consumption in the GNP in order to step up the rate of capital accumulation.

The need to specify a mechanism to perform all of these functions is also neglected by the best-known authors who have inspired the New Left. Instead of facing the problem, they usually propose such formulations as this one by Paul Baran: "a society can be developed in which the individual would be formed, influenced, and educated . . . by a system of rationally planned production for use, by a universe of human relations determined by and oriented toward solidarity, cooperation, and freedom."[3] Or, as Baran has also said, optimal uses of resources in a planned economy "represent a considered judgement of a socialist community guided by reason and science."[4] Others have commented simply that production should be directed toward the "true" needs of the individual and not toward the *wants* expressed in the marketplace.[5] Such formulations are typical of what we find in New Left literature about allocation problems. The Holy Bible conveys almost as much information on criteria for the allocation of resources in an economy in which information is assumed not to be supplied in markets by the spending decisions of the consumers

---

[2]See Assar Lindbeck, "On the Efficiency of Competition and Planning," in Richard Portes, ed., *Planning and Market Relations*, International Economics Association (London: Macmillan, 1971).

[3]Paul Baran, *The Political Economy of Growth* (New York: Monthly Review Press, 1968), p. xvii.

[4]*Ibid.*, p. 42.

[5]See, for instance, Mandel, 2:608.

themselves and where decisions are not coordinated by competition in markets. Nowhere are we told how to find out about the "true needs" for consumer goods. And what criteria should be used for the export sector (which constitutes more than half of the manufacturing sector in many European economies): the "true needs" of foreigners?

Among the "anarchistic" wing of the New Left, the idea is presumably that economic decisions should be undertaken in about the same way as they are made in a democratic family in a primitive subsistence economy. The ideal seems to be some kind of "council democracy," in which people are supposed to convince one another or in which decisions are taken by general vote. It is possible that such a model would function in an agrarian society consisting of a number of rather isolated Robinson-Crusoe economies. However, it is an industrial society we live in, and the complexities inherent in the process of production and exchange not only call for specialization within individual firms but also presuppose that information is obtained regarding the wishes of millions of individuals *outside* the separate decision-making institutions and finally requires that billions of decisions by millions of different units be coordinated and made consistent. In a system of this type, central administrative planning and markets—or rather, various combinations of these two methods—are the only appropriate alternatives we know of.

Related to this flaw in New Left thinking is the notion that the bureaucracy in the Soviet Union is to be regarded as almost an unfortunate accident brought about by the wishes of the bureaucrats themselves and the idiosyncracies of particular individuals, such as Lenin or, more often, Stalin. In fact, as I understand the issue, the large bureaucracy in the Soviet Union (although not necessarily all the *methods* used by it) is an unavoidable consequence of attempts to replace markets by administrative decisions. If economic decisions are not coordinated by markets, they have to be coordinated by central administrative bodies. New Left writers avoid the real problems of the economic system by not realizing that they have, in reality, to choose between markets and centralized administrative procedures, or various combinations of these two methods.

Among some individual authorities of the New Left it is sometimes admitted, however, that a market system "unfortunately" may be necessary for some time even under socialism. An example of this is the stand taken by Paul Sweezy: "The view I hold is that market relationships, which of course imply money and prices, are inevitable under socialism for a long time, but that they constitute a standing danger to the system and unless strictly hedged in and controlled will lead to degeneration and retrogression."[6] However, even Sweezy seems to have argued that market relations and exchange in markets should later be eliminated: "the evolution of socialism into communism requires an unremitting struggle against the principle [of "equivalent exchange"] with a view to its ultimate replacement by the ideal *from* each according to his ability, *to* each according to his needs."[7]

In general, the New Left neglects, or is unaware of, the development of the theory of socialist planning which was largely inspired by the Lange-Lerner model for decentralized market socialism developed during the thirties. Similarly, New Left critics have not incorporated into their thinking the analysis of the techniques of economic planning in socialist as well as in capitalist market systems

[6]Paul Sweezy, "Reply to Charles Bettleheim," *Monthly Review* (March 1969).

[7]Paul Sweezy and Paul Baran, *Monopoly Capital* (New York: Monthly Review Press, 1968), p. 337.

developed by academic economists in both the East and the West during the postwar period.

In this respect, the New Left is to some extent confronted with the same dilemma as is the communist faction of the old Left, which traditionally has argued that bureaucracy is in fact a result of the capitalist market system, with the inference that the state would "wither away" in communist society. This notion, that the state would "wither away" in a system where resources would no longer be allocated by markets, but in fact by public administrative processes, is one of the most puzzling ideas in the history of economic and political doctrine.

The belief that the need to specify a mechanism for the allocation of resources and for the coordination of economic decisions can be neglected is probably strengthened among those reading and accepting the analysis in John Kenneth Galbraith's *The New Industrial State.* In his book Galbraith does not seem to have considered it necessary to explain the mechanism by which the activities of millions of different households and firms—or even of a few hundred very large corporations—are coordinated in the several million different markets in which they operate. By talking about planning *within* firms, and after having declared the market system dead, Galbraith gives innocent readers the impression that an economy characterized by planning *within* large firms is in fact a "planned economy." In Galbraith's world, it would seem that we need neither markets nor central administrative planning. Adam Smith's "Invisible Hand" is replaced by invisible central planners, baptized the "technostructure."

Obviously, economists have not yet been very successful in communicating to the New Left or to the general public, for that matter, either the need for *some* mechanism to allocate resources and coordinate decisions or an understanding of what work the market mechanism in fact performs in this respect. It seems that the work carried out by the market system is taken so much for granted that most people do not reflect very much about it, except when something goes wrong in the system.

Maybe the most effective way to teach the noneconomist about the issue of allocation and the functioning of the market system is to describe the problems which occur when markets have been more or less removed from the mechanism of allocation, such as, for example, when rigid price controls have been introduced. The general experience of rent control in various countries is, I believe, instructive. The effects of rent control have in fact been exactly what can be predicted from the simplest type of supply-and-demand analysis—"housing shortage" (excess demand for housing), black markets, privileges for those who happen to have a contract for a rent-controlled apartment, nepotism in the distribution of the available apartments, difficulties in getting apartments for families with children, and, in many places, deterioration of the housing stock. In fact, next to bombing, rent control seems in many cases to be the most efficient technique so far known for destroying cities, as the housing situation in New York City demonstrates.

It does not seem that New Left students in various parts of the world have shown much understanding of these aspects of price control, for they have made control of rents one of their main, concrete short-run proposals. After seeing how low-income families in the rent-controlled city of Stockholm have waited in the official queue for apartments for five to eight years, while high-income families always can get apartments through good "contacts" or the black market, it is difficult to see the virtues of rent control as a tool of social policy. Similar examples of the social effects of the removal or crippling of markets can be drawn from other fields as well.

Another way to illustrate the role of market systems is to describe problems arising from experiments with administrative controls in communist countries. Even though these countries have succeeded in generating economic growth, they have also been confronted by very much the same problems that are generated by price control in capitalist countries, though of course on a very much larger scale. They have encountered shortages of commodities and the resulting queues; the "seller's markets" and the consequent absence of incentives for producers to provide quality, service, and the development of new products.

The difficulties of adjusting production to demand considerations in administered economic systems are illustrated by a cartoon in the Soviet periodical *Crocodile*. The drawing shows some 100 men pulling an enormous cart, on which rests a nail 100 yards long and 30 yards thick. Onlookers ask what the nail is going to be used for. The answer is "We don't know, but it fulfills our entire quota of 50 tons of nails." The point in the cartoon is, of course, not that administrators in the Soviet Union are stupid but that it is extremely difficult to allocate and coordinate resources and to achieve adjustment to the wishes of buyers in a complicated industrial society without a heavy reliance on markets.

In recent years as these difficulties have been discussed fairly openly in Eastern Europe and as some communist countries have started to move in the direction of market systems, it is ironic that in Eastern Europe it is considered progressive and even radical to advocate greater reliance on markets, at the same time that in the West young radicals regard their opposition to the market system as an important part of their ideology, *in principle*.

An important point in the evaluation of market systems is of course the manner in which preferences are formed, an issue on which the New Left has mounted an attack. There is a strong tendency among New Leftists to argue, as do Galbraith, Marcuse, and some other authors, that preferences are in fact arbitrarily "fabricated" by firms through the production, advertisement, and sales operations themselves, with the implication often made explicit that there is therefore no reason to tailor relative outputs to prevailing preferences. Marcuse, for instance, has declared that as long as individuals "are indoctrinated and manipulated (down to their very instincts), their answer [to the question about their "true" needs] cannot be taken as their own."[8] This refusal to accept household preferences as expressed in market behavior is typical of a very large fraction of the New Left. Characteristic formulations assert that man and his preferences and opinions are formed by the outputs and products and that demand nowadays is adjusted to supply, rather than the reverse.[9]

In a trivial sense, it is of course perfectly true that

[8]Marcuse, p. 6.

[9]In the context of the terminology of economic theory, we might say that the stronger version of this position is a new form of the celebrated Say's Law, according to which "supply creates its own demand." However, whereas Say's Law is alleged to hold for the economy as a whole, the New Left seems, according to this "strong" interpretation, to apply Say's Law to individual products and individual firms: firms are said to be able quite easily (that is, at low cost) to create markets for whatever products they decide to produce. It is not clear, then, how a number of New Left authors or those who have inspired them (for example, Baran and Sweezy) can at the same time believe that there is a permanent tendency in capitalist societies for aggregate demand to rise more slowly than does supply, causing permanent tendencies to unemployment and stagnation—this in spite of the assumed ability of individual firms to "create" the necessary demand for their products. The "inconsistency" would be lessened, however, by putting a "weaker" interpretation on the thesis, that is, by claiming that only *some* industries and firms have this ability to create the necessary demand. But then, why do not these firms drive all others out of the market?

demands for products are "created" by supplying the products on markets—in the sense that people would hardly demand products which they have never seen or heard about. People might have general, though vague and unspecified, preferences for food, clothing, shelter, and sex. But certainly nobody would specifically dream about General Foods peanut butter, Lord and Taylor dresses, Levitt houses, and Vilgot Sjöman's *I Am Curious (Yellow)* if these products had not been put on the market. It is difficult to see why it would be less important to satisfy such demands than to satisfy those that are "spontaneous" in the sense that people would want to buy the products even if they were not on the market—if such products really exist (possibly, breast-milk is an example). For instance, practically all cultural and artistic products—from Beethoven to the Beatles—would then fall into the category of less important and "manipulated" wants.

The idea that there are "true" needs, in contrast to the "false" wants that people actually express and that false wants are created by manipulation, is often transplanted to the political sphere as well. Marcuse has provided an example in his argument that "democracy would appear to be the most efficient system of domination."[10] Obviously, this way of arguing is very close to the general attack on Western democracies launched by totalitarian movements, particularly during the 1920s and 1930s.

Is there any empirical material that can shed some light on the formation of preferences and in particular on the effects of advertising? Unfortunately, as was indicated in the beginning of the book, the scientific studies of the effects of advertising are basically weak. If it were true, however, that sufficient demand could be created for prac-

[10]Marcuse, p. 52.

tically any product that a firm decided to produce simply by advertising, it might be difficult to explain why firms spend so much money to study the potential markets for new products. The purpose of such "prelaunch" studies is, after all, to obtain information about consumer attitudes toward potential new products.

Available studies also indicate that most products that product-development departments regard as "technically successful developments" are never launched on the market because of negative results in market research and market tests. The scanty evidence available also suggests that a very large fraction of the new products that are actually launched on markets fail, despite often extensive advance market studies. A rather usual comment in the literature is that between one-third and one-half of all products put on the market are considered failures by the sponsoring firms, in the sense that they withdraw the product from the market within one year. Among products regarded by the management as "technical successes" only a few, possibly 10 to 20 percent, survive market studies and prelaunch testing and so are launched commercially. Available death-rate figures for new firms also indicate that a considerable fraction—maybe as much as one-half of the new businesses—go bankrupt within one year. (It may be claimed that these firms are mainly small, with limited ability to influence preferences; on the other hand, available studies indicate that decreasing returns to scale for advertising occur at a rather low expenditure level.[11])

Even if these studies are not very comprehensive, the

[11]For bibliographies of the literature in this field, see "New Product Development and Sale," *Small Business Administration*, no. 4 (1963); and P. Doyle, "Economic Aspects of Advertising: A Survey," *Economic Journal* (1968), pp. 570–602. See also Booz, Allen, and Hamilton, Inc., *Management of New Products* (New York, 1966).

results do not seem to support a *strong* hypothesis about the all-powerful effects of advertising on the overall composition of consumption. On the other hand, advertising may have substantial effects on how consumption of a certain type of commodity is divided among different brands, though the effects of advertising by individual firms to some extent cancel out for the market as a whole. It also seems that in most countries studied the pattern of consumer expenditure is related in very much the same way to incomes and relative prices, despite differences in the structure of domestic production and the volume and technique of advertising.[12] The situation is different, of course, in countries such as the Soviet Union, where the government decides on the supply of commodities more independently of the demand situation. However, the impressive queues for exactly those commodities for which we would expect higher demands in the Soviet Union on the basis of Western preferences—mainly durable consumer goods—indicate that household preferences in the Soviet Union may not differ so very much from those in capitalist countries. Interview studies of consumer preferences in the Soviet Union seem to have yielded similar results.

Statistics on profits may supply some additional information about the ability of firms to control their markets. We know that profits differ considerably both among branches and firms, and also for different products within individual firms. I believe that these data do not support

[12]See, for instance, T. Watanable, "A Note on the International Comparison of Private Consumption Expenditure," *Weltwirtschaftliches Archiv*, band 88 (1962); and H. S. Houthakker and L. D. Taylor, *Consumer Demand in the United States, 1929–1970* (Cambridge, Mass.: Harvard University Press, 1966). See also reference in Edward F. Denison and J. P. Poullier, *Why Growth Rates Differ: Postwar Experience in Nine Western Countries* (Washington, D.C.: Brookings Institution, 1967), chap. 17.

the idea that individual firms can by themselves easily determine their profit levels, as often (but not always) is asserted in New Left literature. It would be strange if certain firms voluntarily had chosen zero or negative profits, while other firms obtain profits of more than 20 percent (of the value of equity capital). We also know that profits of individual firms vary considerably over time (aside from variations connected with the general business cycle).

The exaggerations by the New Left, as well as by Marcuse and Galbraith, about the effects of advertising should, of course, not prevent us from seeing the formation of preferences (e.g., the effects of advertising), as an important and serious problem for *any* economic system. First of all, it is quite likely that the volume of advertising today is much higher than is necessary to supply the factual information that it incorporates. This means, of course, that part of this advertising is "economic waste," possibly amounting to one or a few percent of GNP. Some part of product differentiation, as well as frequent model changes, presumably also represent economic waste, particularly in highly monopolized sectors where the freedom of choice for the consumer is particularly restricted. It is also possible, although we do not know for sure, that a lower volume of advertising would lead to lower preferences for consumer goods as compared to public goods, leisure time, and appreciation of the environment. However, it is also possible that a lower volume of "advertising" by politicians, journalists, and writers for public goods and a good environment would reduce people's preferences for these "utilities." In fact, politicians may to a large extent be regarded as advertisers and entrepreneurs in the field of public goods and the environment, which in fact may be regarded as an important part of their function in society. In some capitalist countries, such as the Scandinavian countries, politicians even seem to have achieved wide public support for a rather substantial level of public consumption. In Sweden, for instance, nearly 30 percent of total consumption goes into this sector. In view of this experience, it does not seem to be impossible, as New Left writers sometimes assert, to obtain a rather high level of public consumption in capitalist countries; for instance, André Gorz claims that "collective needs are thus objectively in contradiction to the logic of capitalist development."[13]

The basic problem probably is this: Why should large corporations, politicians, successful authors, and artists have such disproportionate power (as compared to other groups) to influence opinions and preferences? Or, more constructively formulated: Is it possible to form "counter-vailing power" to the power of these groups?

The conventional liberal–social democratic answer to the problem of advertising has, of course, always been to fight monopolies, to improve education about consumer goods, to create independent institutes for consumer research and information, to enact government laws and regulations against dangerous products and false and misleading advertising, and the like. Until such measures have been tried on a large scale it is probably impossible to express a valid opinion on their potential effectiveness. However, I believe that nobody with knowledge and concern about fraud, misleading information, and consumer ignorance would deny the need for more countervailing power in this field.

If the volume of advertising is generally considered too high, a tax on advertising might also be an efficient method to bring it down. One problem is, of course, that the volume

[13]André Gorz, *Strategy for Labor* (Boston: Beacon Press, 1967), p. 94.

of useful information incorporated in advertisements, would simultaneously fall. A more drastic step would be the prohibition of all advertising and its replacement by dissemination by public agencies of information on consumer goods. Even if this solution were administratively possible without considerable bureaucratization, which I doubt, it is questionable whether most people would consider such an arrangement desirable in principle, for it would mean that producers would not be allowed to stand up for their own products. Some public administrators would acquire the power to decide just what information the general public should be exposed to—obviously leading to a very strong centralization of information in society. In the political arena, adherents of democracy will probably argue that it is preferences *after*, rather than *before*, exposure to propaganda and discussion that should count. The same argument can presumably be applied to the marketplace, but one main difference is that there are practically no institutions in present society that oppose various products in the same way that some political parties try to limit the expansion of public spending, for example. Information about products tends to become a monologue rather than a dialogue. It is, of course, for this very reason that the need for the creation of "countervailing powers" in the marketplace is so strong.

There is also a strong tendency in New Left literature to argue as if information could be distributed without cost. Typical is Baran and Sweezy's practice of including all activities that provide information, and even distribution of commodities, in the waste account on the economic balance sheet. (From this point of view, not only advertising agencies but also political parties presumably are regarded as belonging to the wasteful part of the economy.)

In the New Left's criticism of the market system, the

well-known market failures are, of course, also pointed out: the inability of a market system, unaided by economic policy, to achieve economic stability (full employment and stable prices); its inability automatically to guarantee social security and an acceptable distribution of income, wealth, and economic power; its inability to provide collective goods and to handle externalities such as various kinds of pollution without deliberate government policies; and so on.

These well-known limitations of market systems create the need for a public sector and public policies, and they have stimulated attempts to build up a Welfare State. *In general*, however, the New Left in comparison to other groups, has hardly shown extraordinary interest in improving the Welfare State. Practical programs for progressive taxation, social security, income redistribution, public consumption, and action against pollution of various kinds have rather been the domain of the liberal–social democratic supporters of the Welfare State. As a matter of fact, it is easy to find a rather scornful attitude in New Left literature toward the idea of a capitalist Welfare State. Sometimes this attitude seems to reflect a critical feeling toward the state in general, presumably partly a heritage from the Marxist theory of the state as a tool for the repression of workers by the capitalists. For example, Marcuse has argued that the Welfare State is "a state of unfreedom."[14] The idea that workers are repressed by the modern Welfare State, a notion quite consistent with the Marxist theory of the state, surely must sound somewhat paradoxical to labor parties in Western Europe, which, though often opposed by the richest part of the population, contributed to the establishment of the modern Welfare State. Sometimes it is striking how closely some New Left criticism of the Wel-

---

[14]Marcuse, p. 49.

fare State resembles the old Right's fears that increased powers to public authorities would bring the end of individual freedom. This partial convergence of the New Left with the old Right seems, however, to be more characteristic of the American than the European scene. The antipathy toward government is so strongly shared by the extreme (libertarian) Right and part of the New Left that the line heads back on itself and joins a circle, with the extremes meeting. Thus, a pseudonymous writer of the Chicago laissez faire school could, by using a flamboyant style of the New Left, sprinkled with four-letter words, give an image of a New Left book.[15]

To some extent, New Left criticism of the Welfare State may also be a heritage from the classical dilemma of revolutionary socialism, where there has always tended to be a conflict between short-run and the long-run perspectives. If a Welfare State is established within the capitalist society, and many of the injustices and insecurities are thereby removed, how can a climate be created suitable for the overthrow of the system in the long run?

CENTRALIZATION VERSUS DECENTRALIZATION
Related to the problem of the choice between markets and bureaucracy, though not quite the same issue, is the choice between decentralization and centralization. An obvious link between these two problems is, of course, the fact that a market system is consistent with relatively far-reaching decentralization, whereas in a nonmarket system decisions have to be coordinated by some central authority. In fact,

[15]See Angus Black, *A Radical's Guide to Economic Reality* (New York: Holt, Rinehart and Winston, 1970). This tract, which at first reading seems leftish and radical—somewhere on the anarchistic wing of the New Left—gradually reveals itself to be of the Milton Friedman persuasion.

a market economy may be considered mainly as a method of achieving decentralization in economic systems, while at the same time bringing about coordination of economic decisions. *Thus, the more we like decentralization, the more we should favor market systems.* This relation between market systems and decentralization means that much of the discussion in the previous section is relevant here, and so it is possible to be rather brief now.

When economists advocate a heavy reliance on decentralized market systems with competing firms, they usually mention the high costs of collecting and processing information in highly centralized systems, as compared to those in market systems (in which changes in prices and in the quantities demanded transmit the necessary information to producers and consumers). Economists have also sometimes suggested that in systems based on central administrative processes some types of undistorted information may be virtually unobtainable at *any* cost. As regards consumer preferences, this conclusion, of course, follows directly from the theory of the subjective nature of individual preferences. However, there are also enormous difficulties on the production side because of the heterogeneity of products and production processes, which make *specific* knowledge about "time and place" crucial for rational decisions and hence for economic efficiency.

These circumstances constitute a great difficulty not only for central determination of commodity flows in nonmarket systems ("command economies") but also for centrally prescribed prices (as in Oscar Lange's well-known model for "market socialism"). In the latter system, central determination of prices requires knowledge and control of individual product qualities; otherwise, producers of both consumers' and producers' goods can always lower the quality of products whose prices are centrally determined, as has in fact happened in most countries during periods of price control.

A main inference from these observations is, in my judgment, that the possibilities for computers *replacing* decentralized competition in markets in the handling of information and the working out of approximations to optimal allocations, are rather limited. For information systems using instruments other than prices determined by markets are inefficient in communicating such complicated messages as preferences, product qualities, and descriptions of production processes. That computers cannot replace markets in *generating* information (about consumer preferences and production technology) and in *creating* incentives for efficient operation in conformity with consumer preferences is, of course, even more obvious. Clearly, these statements are no denial of the fact that computers can be very useful tools for the kind of central planning which serves as an important complement to the market mechanism in most countries—using data generated both by markets and other processes.

A specific problem affecting centralized administrative processes, designed to direct in detail the allocation of resources, particularly in complex economies, is that these processes in reality imply several "layers" of administrative bodies between the firm and the top decision-makers. When information is "filtered" through these layers, it may be a reasonable hypothesis that most of the information is lost and that part of what remains is distorted, for the reasons mentioned earlier. The more details that are decided at the top, the more serious, of course, is this loss of detailed knowledge.

The problem is accentuated by the fact that administrative hierarchies in reality are, and probably have to be, *pyramids:* The number of persons *receiving* information from below are much fewer than the number of those who *emit* information. Consequently, people at the top of the pyramid can devote only a very small fraction of their time to problems that are analyzed and considered very carefully at lower levels. Moreover, the enormous mass of information and decisions at the top level means that "unqualified" officials in the high-level administrative bodies ("assistants"), in fact, have to make the decisions, even though their general qualifications (hence not only their specific information) are often low as compared to those of the most qualified officials in the low-level units (for example, in firms). Thus, not only is information lost and distorted "on the way" through various administrative layers, but also most decisions may in fact be made by people with lower general qualifications than if the decisions instead had been made at the level of the firms.

Obviously, deficiencies in information and coordination are not confined to central administrative systems. Decentralized systems also suffer from inadequate information and coordination. For instance, in decentralized systems there is an obvious risk that macroinformation (information about the economy as a whole, sometimes available to high-level administrative bodies) is not known or considered at the level of the firm. Individual firms may thus plan according to unrealistic and inconsistent assumptions about the *general* level of economic activity and the growth rate for the economy as a whole, running the risk of temporary overcapacity and various types of macroeconomic instabilities. In market economics this means that coordination of investment decisions might thus be improved by a centralized collection of information. This is, of course, one of the main arguments for some kind of "indicative planning" of the kind used in France, Japan and, perhaps to a smaller extent, in the Scandinavian countries.[16]

These considerations are very relevant to an evaluation of the ideas of the New Left; very strong sympathies for decentralization are usually expressed in New Left literature. In this respect, the New Left also deviates from the main tradition of the old Left, which in general was more centralist in its outlook, with more emphasis on central planning. One reason for this difference may be that the young generation today has experienced the problems connected both with tendencies toward centralization in capitalist societies, in large corporations as well as in the state, and the much more far-reaching centralization in most communist countries. However, some of the "older" inspirers of the New Left have also expressed a strong antipathy to centralization, unlike the more "traditional" Marxists such as Maurice Dobb, and to some extent also Baran and Sweezy. An example is Mandel: It is his position that in an economy which is characterized by "planned bureaucracy and centralized fashion . . . sacrifices are imposed without the victims being asked their views and without obtaining *their prior consent*. Such a system of management is contrary to the principles of socialism, and furthermore it leads to economic results which are inferior to those of a more democratic system of management."[17]

One basic dilemma for the New Left which, however, is not brought out clearly in the New Left literature, is that its strong sympathy for decentralization is difficult to reconcile with its rejection of the market system, which presumably is the only type of economic system that permits far-reaching decentralization in complex industrial societies.

[16]See Lindbeck, "On the Efficiency of Competition and Planning."
[17]Mandel, 2:631.

The dilemma is complicated further by the fact that some New Leftists—sometimes also just those who favor decentralization—often also advocate more central social and economic planning. In this respect the New Left is to some extent confronted by the same dilemma that faced the syndicalist movement, which also simultaneously emphasized decentralization and central planning.

The classical way of escaping, rather than solving, this type of dilemma is presumably to argue that centralization is necessary in the short run but that in the future society far-reaching decentralization will in fact be implemented—an idea related to the Marxist notion of the "withering away" of the state in the long run. (Another parallel is the tendency for most new military dictatorships to assert that the extraordinary central powers taken today will, in fact, prepare the ground for democratic elections and decentralization in the future.) The idea that central planning will be absent in a future communist society, though rather comprehensive central planning will be necessary in the transitional period between capitalism and socialism and for some time during the stage of socialism, is typical of several New Left authorities, such as Sweezy and Mandel. This temporary centralized planning should, however, be implemented with the enthusiasm and participation of the masses. "Without revolutionary enthusiasm, and mass participation, centralized planning becomes increasingly authoritarian and rigid with resulting multiplication of economic difficulties and failures."[18] On these issues Bakunin was, in my opinion, much more realistic than were the Marxists, when he denied that strengthening the powers of the state, for instance, by means of the "dictatorship of the proletariat,"

[18]Sweezy, "Reply to Charles Bettleheim."

would make possible a later drastic reduction of the powers of the state, as symbolized by the idea of its "withering away."

Finding an optimal combination of centralization and decentralization—and of markets and administrative procedures—is, of course, a *general* problem rather than a problem for the New Left specifically. What makes the dilemma particularly striking for the New Left, however, is that few groups in society are at the same time both so strongly against markets and bureaucracy and so much in favor of decentralization (though sometimes, as indicated, also demanding more central planning).

Presumably these "inconsistencies" are to some extent an expression of the heterogeneity of the movement—in that people with quite different opinions have been given the same label—and, to some extent, it is an illustration of the fact that political positions often are somewhat inconsistent. However, it is possible that the apparent conflict between the demands for decentralization and for central planning in some cases may be resolved by arguing that centralism is present today in many areas where it is scarcely necessary (as in the school system in several European countries) yet absent in many areas where it is most needed (as in the field of conservation and externalities in general)—which happens to be the opinion of the author of this book.

A related characteristic of the New Left movement is its advocacy of decentralization *within* firms and other organizations, often formulated as a criticism of the "hierarchical structure" in decision-making procedures within prevailing organizations, and its related assertions about alienation of employees. Many writers demand more democratic decision-making procedures, sometimes calling for "participatory," or "direct" democracy. Mandel and Gorz are among those who have emphasized "workers' control."[19]

In general, it seems that the New Left has made the lack of democracy in present capitalist societies one of the main targets in its criticism of capitalism. Thus, the old demand for workers' control of factories, or possibly community control, now often supplemented by the demand for student control of universities, has been one of the most characteristic features of the New Left's position, often expressed as a demand for "control of our own lives."

It can hardly be denied that most firms and other organizations in current societies have a hierarchical decision-making structure. Nor is it self-evident that these structures always result in the most efficient way of running organizations. And even if it were the most efficient way, there would, of course, still be the question of whether the gains in efficiency were worth possible, largely unknown, losses of other kinds, such as in "personal satisfaction on the job." From this point of view, there seem to be strong reasons for experimentation with new forms of decision-making structures within various kinds of organizations and also to follow with interest the experiments with more "democratic" decision-making procedures in some countries: for example, workers' councils in Yugoslavia and, on a smaller scale and with more limited tasks, in Norway, where in a few selected firms, there have been experiments with "self-managed" groups of workers, a result of cooperation between employer and employee organizations.

Actually, the issue of more democratic decision-making procedures and workers' participation is, of course, closely connected with the issue of property rights and hence the ownership of the means of production; one important com-

[19]See, for instance, Mandel, 2:644–680; Gorz, pp. 40–50.

ponent of property rights is the choice of decision-making procedures within firms, which may vary considerably even without any change in the *formal* ownership of the means of production. The meaning of "ownership" is quite relative and depends entirely on the laws and administrative practices of the respective countries. This brings us to the next issue—the structure of ownership of the means of production.

OWNERSHIP OF CAPITAL

The New Left has a very egalitarian approach to society, thus following a basic theme in the socialist tradition. As among socialists in general, this leads to strong criticism of the structure of ownership in present societies.

The classical (and possibly the strongest moral and emotional) argument against private capitalism and in favor of collective ownership may be expressed by the rhetorical quest for equality: Why should wealth—and thereby also income and economic power—be as unevenly distributed as it is in present capitalist societies? Personally, I have always regarded this as the main argument in favor of some form of socialism. It has to be admitted, however, that some problems of private capitalism certainly are not solved by collective ownership and that some new problems would certainly arise.

Let us first look at some of the problems of private capitalism that are not solved automatically by public ownership. In present societies, capital in the form of physical and financial assets obviously accounts for only part of the total stock of wealth in the economy. A large and growing part of the capital stock consists of capital in the form of acquired education and training—what in recent years has been baptized "human capital." It seems that the return on human capital today is already more important as an explanation for inequalities in income in the United States than the return on physical and financial capital. In most developed countries, about three-quarters of the national income consists of wage income, the remainder representing interest, rent, and profit. Recent empirical studies for the United States, such as a new (still unpublished) study by Jacob Mincer, indicate that at least two-thirds of the inequalities in wage (and salary) income in the United States can be explained by the distribution of human capital. Thus, assuming that human capital cannot be nationalized (provided slavery is not acceptable!), the nationalization of physical and financial capital would remove only part, and probably a diminishing part, of the total capital stock from private to collective hands. Of course, the nationalization of physical and financial capital by itself would have important, not to say drastic, effects on the distribution of income, wealth, and power in society.

The most obvious substitute for nationalization of human capital is probably nationalization of (part of) the *return* on human capital, for instance by progressive taxation. A much more efficient method, in the long run, is probably an expansion of the educational system to increase the supply of highly educated people, thus influencing wage differentials. However, then we are in the world of conventional liberal-social democratic policies, in which various kinds of inequalities in the distribution of income have always, though not necessarily successfully, been fought in this way (or it has at least been proposed to have them so fought).

Thus, it seems that the application of the concept of human capital, developed by economists such as Theodore Schultz, Gary Becker, and Jacob Mincer, has important implications both for the usefulness of various types of distribution policies and for political ideology. In fact, many New

Leftists themselves, as students investing in human capital, are "capitalists" by this new definition of capital—they own, control, and enjoy the return on capital or will do so later on. Every serious study of the characteristics of capital formation—including the postponement of consumption; the return on earlier expenditure; the control of production processes; and the "power" over other people—shows that there is a precise and fundamental analogy between physical and human capital.

Another problem that is not automatically solved by collective ownership is, of course, the distribution of *power* in society, particularly under a relatively centralized form of collective ownership and management. In several capitalist countries, such as the United States (but probably less so in, for instance, the Scandinavian countries), there is an obvious tendency for economic, political, and military power to be concentrated in the same hands. Certainly this is illustrated by the amazing political power of economically strong and well-organized pressure groups in the United States; with the well-known ability in many cases to bring about legislation in their own favor—tax loopholes, subsidies and protection of agriculture and industry, regulation of certain industries—at the same time that underprivileged minorities are unable to obtain good education, elementary health care, and, in some cases, even sufficient food.

It is quite possible that a society with collective ownership of capital can solve some of these problems by wiping out privileges and helping poor minority groups to attain a decent life, depending on the values, honesty, and altruism of the administrators. It is not very likely, however, that the problem of the distribution of economic and political power will be solved. In the case of a centralist solution of the problem of collective ownership—nationalization—we would expect the problem to be accentuated, for then the bulk of economic power over physical assets would be concentrated in the "one hand" which also happens to exert political and military power: that is, the hand of centrally placed politicians and administrators. For instance, though in some capitalist countries today we have a strong military-industrial complex, sometimes stimulating an aggressive foreign policy, it does not seem convincing to argue that nationalization would necessarily make a country less inclined to use a combination of economic, political, and military force to promote high military spending and an aggressive foreign policy. Milovan Djilas, the former Vice-President of Yugoslavia, has even questioned whether we should really talk about such a thing as "collective" ownership, for in fact there will always be in every system some *individuals* who administer and hence control (and possibly also enjoy the fruits of) the capital stock, which in Djilas' opinion is the essence of "ownership."[20]

The problem of the military-industrial complex seems to be part of a larger problem: Who protects the individual in a society in which political, economic, and military power, to a larger or smaller extent, tend to be in the same hands? This problem is obviously already relevant in the capitalist countries. A typical example, I believe, is the supersonic airplane projects in various countries: Who takes care of the interests of the individual consumer when

[20]Even Sweezy has hinted at this view of "public ownership," though for a system in which economic decisions have been decentralized to the management of enterprises and resources are to a considerable extent allocated by "the impersonal pressure of the market": "Under these circumstances *the juridical form of state property becomes increasingly empty* and real power over the means of production, which is the essence of the ownership concept, gravitates into the hands of the managerial elite" (Sweezy, "Reply to Charles Bettleheim").

two prestige-conscious governments, like those of France and Great Britain, cooperating with two big firms to construct a plane in which probably very few people would want to fly if production costs were not subsidized and if those who will suffer from the sonic boom had to be compensated? It is not likely that this problem would be less acute if governments not only cooperated with private airplane producers, but in fact owned the airplane factories (as they do to some extent in France and Great Britain). Similar examples of emerging symbiosis between government and industry can easily be found in other countries, including the United States: the involvement of the U.S. government in the regulation of the petroleum industry, inventory stocks of various raw materials, atomic energy, missiles, rocketry, and communications satellite systems are cases in point. In these areas, Galbraith's notion of a unified "technostructure" is persuasive.

No doubt there is some awareness among the New Left of the risks inherent in a concentration of power in nationalized economies as expressed both in its sympathy for decentralization and in its criticism of the Soviet system. This holds both for domestic and foreign policy problems. In the more traditional literature of the Left which is Marxist in orientation, by contrast, the risks are often categorically denied. Baran and Sweezy have simply declared that "militarism and conquest are completely foreign to Marxian theory, and a socialist society contains no class or group which, like the big capitalists of the imperialist countries, stands to gain from a policy of subjugating other nations and peoples."[21] For people with knowledge and experience of events after World War II in such countries as Estonia, Latvia, Lithuania, Poland, the eastern sector of Germany,

---

[21]Baran and Sweezy, p. 186.

Czechoslovakia, Hungary, Rumania, and Bulgaria, statements of this sort are probably not easy to accept.

Even when the Marxist theory of imperialism, wars, and racism is not dogmatically put forward in New Left writings, there clearly is a tendency, following the Marxist tradition, to argue as if most bad things in this world, including imperialism, were mainly the result of a particular structure of the ownership of the means of production—of private capitalism. According to Mandel, for instance, socialist planning would, in the long run, bring about "the withering-away of market economy, classes, social inequality, the state, and the division of labour."[22]

Personally, I feel that the correlation between the structure of ownership, on the one hand, and political and social conditions, on the other, is in reality rather vague. Preindustrial and precapitalist societies have certainly been characterized by militarism, aggressive foreign policy, and imperialism—and present-day noncapitalist societies are hardly free of a military-industrial complex and an aggressive nationalist foreign policy! If we were foolish enough to single out *one* factor only to explain imperialistic policies during the last few thousand years, it would seem that the size and economic potential of countries are more important explanatory variables than is the structure of the ownership of the means of production. This hypothesis is consistent with the (reasonable) view that the two main imperialist countries today are the United States and the Soviet Union. This means that an explanation of "imperialism" in terms of "private capitalism" is inadequate: imperialism must rather be attributed to the concentration of economic and political power in certain nations, an illustration of Lord Acton's cynical remark, "Power corrupts; absolute power corrupts absolutely."

[22]Mandel, 2:637.

I would also argue that the New Left underestimates the importance of ideology in the foreign policy of the big powers. Both the Soviet Union's intervention in Czechoslovakia and that of the United States in Vietnam presumably are not devoid of ideological motives—to support communism and anticommunism, respectively—quite apart from the "economic" interests of the two powers. To this, of course, should be added long-term considerations of national security, maybe the crucial consideration.

It seems that domestic political and social conditions too are only vaguely correlated with the structure of ownership of capital. Thus, both the allocation of resources and social conditions—such as the quality of public services and the treatment of minorities—vary considerably among countries with (mainly) nationalized physical capital. Similar variations are to be found in countries with mainly private ownership. Compare, for instance, phenomena such as the level of military spending on defense (and attack!), the existence of slums, social security, the quality of public services, the existence of discrimination, racism, the commitment to redistribution of income, and so on, in different countries with (approximately) the same ownership structure in the industrial sector (90 percent private ownership of the capital in industry, banking, and agriculture), such as the United States and the Scandinavian countries. These dissimilarities in social conditions are partly related to the fact that different countries with the same *formal* structure of ownership, by way of legislation and social and economic policies, have given the concept of ownership different contents.

It is, of course, possible in principle to weaken property rights so much—by giving rights to public authorities, employees, or consumers—that ownership of physical property will not differ much, in terms of economic power, from ownership of government bonds or bank accounts. It is, in my opinion, a fundamental mistake to interpret the rather stationary structure of *formal* ownership in many capitalist countries as an indication that the content of property rights and, hence, of economic power, has not changed much in these countries during recent decades. It is also dubious, I think, to argue as if the distribution of formal ownership were more important than education and political influence in determining economic power.

Of course this does not mean that a far-reaching weakening of property rights can be achieved without various complications and disadvantages. Examples of such difficulties, if the process is driven beyond certain limits, include the risk of unclear division of responsibilities, with a resulting loss of efficiency; strong concentration of power in a small group of politicians and administrators (especially if that group also assumes entrepreneurial and managerial functions); long lines of communication; the risk of heavy bureaucratization; and the like. An important research task for the social sciences—and an important political issue— is the investigation of the likely location of these limits within various fields.

It also seems to follow from the preceding observations that there is some question about the notion, frequently encountered among conservative politicians and social scientists, (see, for example, Friedrich Hayek's famous *The Road to Serfdom*), that nationalization of capital will *necessarily* lead to dictatorship. Historically, the order in which nationalization and dictatorship have occurred seems rather to have been the reverse of that suggested by Hayek. In all communist dictatorships today, dictatorship came first and nationalization afterward, rather than the other way around (except for the Soviet Union, where nationalization and the present form of dictatorship came simultaneously). The same sequence—first dictatorship, later nationalization—

certainly holds also for a number of noncommunist dictatorships with largely nationalized economies (for example, Burma and Syria). There does not seem to be an example of a country where it is reasonable to say that nationalization *resulted* in dictatorship, or that the two had to go together.

This is of course no denial of the possibility that in the future there may be instances where extensive nationalization results in such a strong concentration of power in the hands of government that a changeover to dictatorship is facilitated or generated. To look at the problem from another point of view, it is also quite possible that the introduction of a decentralized market system into a political dictatorship helps to pave the way for decentralization and democratization of the political system as well. This possibility was, in fact, one of the main reasons for the demands for economic reforms in Czechoslavakia during the 1960s— and perhaps also one of the reasons why the reforms were stopped in such a drastic manner. It also seems obvious that the structure of ownership and decision-making within an economy has an important influence on the resources which are available to various political parties for their information and propaganda activities.

Thus, it is absurd to argue that there are *no* relations between economic and political structures. My main point about the limited correlations between economic and political conditions is that the relationships are so complicated that simple generalizations—whether by Hayek or the Marxists—are not convincing. This statement is, of course, not an attempt to minimize the risk of a substantial concentration of power and of a limitation on personal freedom in a society based mainly on public ownership. I think, however, that the more universal risks are bureaucratization, a lack of decentralization of initiative, and a propensity to abstain from criticism of highly placed public officials (for career reasons), rather than dictatorship (in the fascist or communist sense).

Some problems associated with the concentration of power in nationalized economies might, at least in principle, be solved by decentralization of economic powers to the level of the firm. Such a decentralization may, as already indicated, be quite consistent with the New Left sympathies in this regard. It seems that the ideal economic structure in much of New Left writing is an economy of autonomous (possibly rather small), firms, owned and operated by the employees themselves—a kind of producers' cooperative, or "collective capitalism." Mandel talks about "self-management of free communes of producers and consumers, in which everybody will take it in turn to carry out administrative work, in which the difference between 'directors' and 'directed' will be abolished, and a federation which will eventually cover the whole world."[23] A great many such firms were in fact started on the European continent during the second half of the nineteenth century and the early years of the present century. The traditional explanation of their inability to compete with capitalist firms is that they never succeeded in solving the management problems, and possibly also the problems of accumulating capital and finance in general.

However, to make decentralization possible in complex industrial systems, it is necessary, as was already pointed out, to rely rather heavily on markets. From that point of view it is certainly of interest to note that the trend in Eastern Europe toward greater reliance on markets is combined with attempts to achieve decentralization down to the level of the firm (still within the context of public ownership). But we do not yet know if politicians and central

[23]Mandel, 2:672.

administrators in these countries are really willing to give up the powers they acquired in the previous centralized administrative economic system. A dilemma involved in bringing about far-reaching decentralization in economies dominated by collective ownership is that it is just those who hold political power who can decide *if* they want to abstain from this power or not. Under private capitalism, a considerable distribution of power is more or less automatically achieved when the ownership of capital is not concentrated in the hands of one or a few individuals or firms. Thus, a serious conflict easily emerges between the wish to reach decentralization and the desire for public (particularly government) ownership.

Let us assume, however, that it will in fact be possible to create societies characterized by decentralized market socialism, possibly combined with democratic institutions. What problems will remain? First of all, the problems of economic instability, distribution of wage income, and externalities will not be very different from corresponding problems in capitalist societies. As a matter of fact, short-run investment cycles do not seem to be smaller in most East European "socialist" countries than in capitalist Western Europe. And problems of inflation seem to arise, quite regardless of the structure of ownership, as soon as some modest degree of decentralization of price and wage formation occurs. Note, for instance, the rapid rising rates of inflation in Yugoslavia and Czechoslovakia during the experiments with market socialism. Moreover, the ability in different economic systems to take efficient action against negative external effects on the environment seems to be rather independent of the actual economic system; perhaps the most important prerequisite for such action is, in fact, an interested and active public opinion and, hence, free debate.

A more *specific* problem for socialist market economies

seems to be designing ways for individuals to take *new* initiatives (such as the development of new products, new firms, and new production techniques) when private ownership in the sphere of production is not permitted.

If only those who already have succeeded in reaching the top levels of the prevailing hierarchies are allowed to take initiative, is it not likely that initiative will be hampered? People who already have top posts may often be concerned mainly with the risk of losing them, which means, in fact, a high risk aversion; the most efficient method to minimize this risk may be to avoid new adventures. It is not obvious that such problems can be avoided in a less hierarchical system of organizations *within* firms (for instance, with voting rights and majority decision-making for all employees). In this case too, it may be difficult to launch new ventures if on every occasion the majority has to be convinced that a new product is worth producing and a new method of production worth applying. Another complication is the difficulty of convincing the majority in a firm that a plant should be moved to another region or possibly be closed down completely. We need more information about these problems, and this presumably requires practical experiments.

It can hardly be denied that to a considerable extent capitalist systems have solved these problems, as anybody who can put together the necessary capital is allowed to try a project in which neither the managers of established firms, the politicians, nor the majority of the employees within existing firms believe. Modern empirical research on the process of innovation in capitalist countries seems to indicate that technological progress in fact rests on thousands, not to say millions, of individual decisions. The studies also indicate that "outsiders," quite frequently *new* firms or foreign firms, often introduce the real "big new" commodities and production processes into a country. (For instance, how could the New Left itself have evolved had individuals not had the right to establish new periodicals and publishing firms without a permit from public authorities?)

This problem—of encouraging initiatives—is probably the basic unsolved problem of completely (or largely) nationalized economies, along with the problem of avoiding bureaucratization and a strong concentration of economic, political, and military power in the same hands. An area where public ownership is quite likely to result in an improvement, according to usual values, as compared to private ownership, is, of course, the distribution of income from physical and financial assets.

MATERIAL INCENTIVES AND DISTRIBUTION PROBLEMS

In general, the New Left attitude toward material incentives—by way of profits as well as wage differentials—is quite negative. This reflects, of course, the egalitarian leanings of the New Left movement and, perhaps also, the tendency toward "economic puritanism" which is characteristic of part of the movement. Instead, "moral incentives" and, in the long run, the creation of "a new man" (à la the beliefs of Guevara) are emphasized.

Thus, the New Left is not very inclined to use wage differentials as incentives for efficiency, education, and training, or as a method of allocating labor to different jobs. This element in the program of the New Left is very significant, for the only *realistic* alternative to economic incentives may be—and in the opinion of practically all economists *is*—government conscription and hence the abolishment of the freedom of the individual to choose a profession (in competition with others). It should be noted, however, that it is possible (though we do not know this) that today's wage differentials in many countries are larger than what can be defended from the point of view of efficiency and allocation. Probably a more important point is that the wage differentials of today reflect the present distribution of human capital. It should be possible, through a more egalitarian distribution of investment in human capital, to achieve a more even distribution also of wage and salary incomes.

The New Left is particularly energetic in its criticism of profits, which usually are regarded, in accordance with the Marxist theory of value, as a form of exploitation. Consequently, high profits in certain sectors and firms are not considered as a possible sign of great efficiency or as an acceptable incentive for expansion of production in these areas. On the contrary, high profits are considered as a sign of particularly great exploitation, even when firms which earn high profits because of their efficiency also happen to pay relatively good wages (which is often the case). Thus, profits seem to be regarded mainly as a form of income transfer—which it must be admitted is *one* aspect of profits, at least in monopolistic market situations.

Obviously, an underlying notion is that allocation of resources in accordance with profit prospects is not socially acceptable. This position is usually not explicitly explained, but rather is taken as an axiom in such formulations as "production should be directed according to needs rather than maximum profits." Very seldom is it understood that the relevant question is not profits *versus* needs, but rather that the issue is to what extent a market economy based on the profit motive *does or does not* achieve production and allocation of resources in accordance with desired criteria, such as the preferences of the individual.

As economists have long since tried to show, it is very

difficult to find a better *criterion* for efficiency in the allocation of resources, in accordance with given consumer preferences, than that of production being directed according
to profit prospects—provided that a reasonable degree of
competition exists and that the supply of collective goods
and the problem of externalities are taken care of in one
way or another (in practice, by government policies). The
simple reason is, of course, that profits are a measure of
the difference between the value of the result of production
and the value of productive resources used. It has also
proved difficult to find better *incentives* for moving in the
direction of such an efficient allocation of resources and
for improving production technique and product qualities.

Obviously, the same observations lie behind the new
tendencies in Eastern Europe and the Soviet Union to make
profit maximization the main goal, or one of the main goals,
of individual firms in the increasingly decentralized market
system which seems to be emerging in some of these countries. A parable from Soviet agriculture illustrates the
point. Farm labor was at first compensated in proportion
to the acreage plowed and sowed. As a consequence, plow-
ing was done more speedily than carefully, and the distance
between each seed was large. To improve efficiency, the
authorities decided to pay in proportion to the output of
the land, with the result that the farmers used all factors
of production they could get hold of, as long as output rose,
regardless of the costs involved. To give farmers an incentive to economize, that is, to balance output against costs,
the authorities then got the idea of paying the farmers on
the basis of the difference between the value of output and
the costs of production. Of course, this difference is nothing
other than the profit. Even if this parable is not an au-
thentic description of the way in which the profit motive
was rediscovered in the Soviet Union, it probably gives an

intuitive feeling of why the profit level of firms is relevant both as a criterion of, and as an incentive to, efficiency within firms.

The new economic developments in Eastern Europe, particularly the restoration of markets and the profit motive, are usually not well received in New Left literature. In this sense, the New Left may be characterized as rather "pure" inheritors of the Marxian theory of value, because of its critical attitude to profits even in societies where profits are not received by private property owners. From this point of view, the tendency in Eastern Europe (for instance in Hungary) to pay bonuses out of profits to the managers of nationalized firms must be disturbing, as such payments in fact are very similar to dividend payments to managers with stocks in capitalist firms (as long as the managers of nationalized firms are not fired).

As is well known, the notion of profits as a form of exploitation sometimes leads to somewhat paradoxical results. For instance, highly paid employees in government administration and large corporations (without shares in the firms) are to be considered as exploited, whereas low-income owners of small firms with small profits are exploiters. Following this line of reasoning a few years ago, some "radical" students in Sweden found it logical to support a strike by high-income professional groups (including university professors), whereas some liberal and social democratic students were against the strike on the grounds that the strikers constituted a high-income group who, according to their principles of equality, should abstain from wage increases.

Thus, a consistent Marxist approach to distribution problems may, as illustrated by these examples, lead to rather restricted views on problems of the distribution of income, by supporting all kinds of wage increases regardless of how high the income of the particular groups in fact already is. From a logical point of view, this problem might be "solved" by including human capital in the concept of the capital stock; then it would have to be admitted, however, that all problems of control, return, and enjoyment of capital cannot be solved by nationalization of physical and financial capital.

A classic problem for Marxist theory has been to reconcile the theory of pauperization of workers with the empirical data. As was noted by Marxists at the end of the nineteenth century, a theory proclaiming an *absolute* reduction in workers' incomes over time was not consistent with empirical evidence, which indicated that there had been a rather continuous rise in the standard of living for workers during the process of industrialization. A new theory was developed, therefore, according to which the living standard of workers was said not to be falling in absolute terms but, instead, falling in relation to that of the capitalists—the theory of relatively rising exploitation. During the course of this century, it has become rather clear, however, that available statistical data does not support this theory either, for the shares of profits and wages in the national income seem to have been rather stable in the long run in most of the developed countries studied; in fact in some cases, particularly after World War II, a tendency to a rising share of wages has been observed.

Baran and Sweezy have recently made a new attempt to reconcile the idea of rising exploitation with available empirical data, an attempt not infrequently referred to in New Left literature. Instead of profits, Baran and Sweezy talk about the "surplus," which includes not only profits, rent, and interest but also that part of private investment which is not financed out of profits, plus all public consumption and investment (including both the Warfare and the Welfare States) as well as what is called "unnecessary consumption." Thus, even though the concept of the surplus sounds rather similar to the Marxist "surplus value," it is considerably broader, and more heterogeneous, in scope.

Analytically, the surplus is defined as the difference between the maximum GNP possible with available resources (hence with full-capacity utilization) and "necessary consumption." We are told that this surplus, obviously meant to be a measure mainly of "waste" and "exploitation," was 56.1 percent of GNP in the United States in 1963 and that it has been rising for a long time (of course, the fraction of national income devoted to public consumption and investment has been continuously rising in recent decades in most countries). Many adherents of the Welfare State may no doubt be surprised to find that public schools, hospitals, and other parts of the Welfare State are included in this surplus, along with "waste" and "exploitation." Even though Baran and Sweezy probably are not opposed to welfare arrangements in capitalist societies, the inclusion of these activities in the surplus is not inconsistent with the Marxist theory of the state, according to which this institution is only a tool for capitalists to exploit workers. Similarly, it is right in line with Marxist theory to regard the activities of administrators in the public sector as a nonproductive waste of resources, because this type of labor, to quote Baran, "is bound gradually to disappear as a socialist society advances in the direction of communism" (in spite of the fact that resources in such a society shall not be allocated by way of markets).[24] Some people will also find it difficult to decide what is "necessary" and what is "unnecessary" consumption—particularly for other people.

Another difficult problem, and one that is a *general* dilemma

[24]Baran, p. 33.

rather than specific to the New Left, is that the desire for decentralization sometimes comes into conflict with the desire for equality. Far-reaching decentralization, as for instance in collective bargaining and public administration, easily results in considerable differentials in living standards among regions and possibly also among professions. The centralization of collective bargaining in some countries and the attempts by central governments to influence and finance local governments, can to a large extent be seen as attempts to equalize the standard of living and the quality of public services in different industries and regions.

Problems also arise when Marxist theories of exploitation are applied by the New Left to problems of underdeveloped countries. The New Left has shown great awareness of problems connected with private investment in underdeveloped countries, such as cases of "unnecessarily" large profits to the investors, political influence of large corporations in small countries, and various aspects of imperialism and neocolonialism. I think the New Left, simply by being suspicious, has here seen more clearly than many other groups the problems arising out of foreign investment in underdeveloped countries. However, a Marxist theory is hardly necessary for the analysis of such problems, and the theory does create a number of unnecessary problems. For instance, criticism by New Leftists of investment in underdeveloped countries tends to be particularly hard where private investment leads to high profits, as if investment by inefficient firms unable to obtain profits (or even incurring losses) would be more advantageous for underdeveloped countries than investment in well-chosen projects or well-run operations which, however, result in high profits. In fact, high profits are in many cases a sign that a project is suitable for a country and that the firm is well managed. Instead of complaining about all investments that give a good return, it might be more constructive to argue for better institutional conditions—such as competition and internationally organized advisory agencies—to help poor countries retain for themselves as much of the profit as possible and also gradually to obtain more domestic control of the operations of the firms. Again, profits seem to be regarded as a transfer payment rather than a criterion of and incentive for efficiency. In New Left literature, market transactions usually seem to be regarded as "zero-sum games": What one partner gains is assumed to be lost by the other, a strong contrast to the economic theory of "comparative advantage."

Another instance in which the exploitation theory creates problems is the assertion that underdeveloped countries are exploited when rich countries buy products from them, particularly when the products are produced by cheap labor. First of all, it is difficult, in applying this theory, to avoid the conclusion that exploitation is performed by practically *all* of us in rich countries, wage-earners as well as capitalists—a disturbing conclusion for an adherent of a Marxist theory of exploitation. Second, the conclusion that we could avoid exploiting underdeveloped countries by stopping imports from them is also disturbing, particularly as the New Left often severely criticizes quotas and tariffs against exports of underdeveloped countries on the ground that their export possibilities are thus undermined.

A non-Marxist concerned about these problems seems to have an intellectually easier position; he can "simply" argue for a removal of tariffs and quotas against exports from underdeveloped countries, for the creation of an international tax-and-transfer system to achieve an income redistribution from rich to poor countries (in the same way that has been attempted within some rich countries), and for steps to ensure that as much as possible of the profit from investment in underdeveloped countries stays within those countries—by more favorable contracts for profit-sharing in the future and by legislation to reduce the risk of domination by private firms or by foreign governments (a risk which can hardly be confined to *private* investments).

COMPETITION

In New Left literature there is much criticism of competition—among both firms and individuals. Basically, the argument against competition seems to be an ethical one: competition is regarded as less moral than cooperation. An alternative society is envisioned, one in which human beings in cooperation and harmony solve common problems, relieved from the stress generated by the rat race in a competitive society. This is, of course, the old utopia of both communists and many religious movements. Competition is also accused of being chaotic, uncoordinated, inefficient, and likely to result in a structure of production not in conformity with the needs of the individual. Sometimes, competition among firms is said to be dead nowadays anyway and so not worth supporting.

In contrast, the achievements of capitalist competition were quite enthusiastically described by Marx: "The bourgeoisie has been the first to show what man's activity can bring about. It has accomplished wonders far surpassing Egyptian pyramids, Roman aqueducts, and Gothic cathedrals. . . . The bourgeoisie, during its role of scarce one hundred years, has created more massive and more colossal productive forces than have all preceding generations together."[25]

It seems that today neo-Marxists and the New Left usually

---

[25]Karl Marx and Friedrich Engels, *The Communist Manifesto*, in *The Essentials of Marx* (New York: Vanguard Press, 1931).

concentrate on the negative aspects of competition in capitalist societies: Uncoordinated investment decisions by competing firms are said to cause violent business cycles; investments selected on the basis of individual advantage are said not to give (maximum) overall benefits to the entire economy; and competition is judged to result in an inferior morale and culture, and so on.[26] In socialist or communist societies, competition is obviously regarded as neither desirable nor necessary. Thus, New Left authorities, such as Mandel, Gorz, Baran, and Sweezy, seem to agree with Engels: "It [communism] will, in other words, abolish competition and replace it with association."[27]

What can an economist say about all this? Of course, we have a static theory of allocation and economic welfare, according to which optimal allocation of resources under certain ideal conditions emerges in a perfectly competitive economy, preferences and technology being regarded as given. There is also a multiperiod allocation theory, in which various limitations of the market solution for investment decisions are analyzed. However, most empirical studies do not indicate that the losses in static efficiency due to production operations below the optimum level in monopolistic firms (the market structure being given) are very large in present-day capitalist economies—maybe one percent of GNP; waste in the form of "unnecessary" sales promotion and model changes has to be added, of course.[28] It is also quite likely that additional economic gains can be obtained in most capitalist countries (though hardly in the United

[26]See, for instance, Mandel, 2:617; Gorz, p. 81.
[27]Friedrich Engels, "Principles for Communism," trans. Paul Sweezy, *Monthly Review* Pamphlet Series (1963).
[28]See, for instance, Harvey Leibenstein, "Allocative Efficiency vs. 'X-Efficiency'," *The American Economic Review* (June 1966); and studies by Arnold Harberger, Edward Denison and others.

States) by a change in the structure of firms to exploit the returns to scale more fully.

I think that this static theory of allocation is useful mainly as a method of understanding and defining the meaning of "the optimum" and to show how very large distortions of relative prices (as compared to opportunity costs) —larger distortions, in fact, than seem to prevail in most developed capitalist economies today, outside of agriculture, public goods, and the environment—can incur very high costs to the economy. However, most applied economists in the field of allocation analysis and industrial organization would presumably argue that the case for competition is more dynamic—that competition *of some sort* (whether perfect, oligopolistic, or monopolistic) among at least a handful of firms creates incentives for resource-saving innovations, product developments, and cost reductions in general. This means that the important thing is probably not whether there is *perfect* competition or not—with individual firms being unable to influence prices—but whether competition of some kind exists (except fraud, predatory price-cutting, and so on), thus stimulating efficiency, innovation, and adjustment to consumer preferences.[29] Personally, I am quite convinced that this is the important aspect of competition. I am, for instance, quite impressed with how changes in routines within firms—changes which are at first regarded as impossible—are suddenly implemented, if a competitive situation forces the firms to do so.

Most economists can probably produce an ample supply of examples of firms whose efficiency increased as a result of increased competitive pressure. Often, particularly in small countries, such pressure can be expected to come

[29]See, for instance, Joe S. Bain, *Industrial Organization*, 2nd ed. (New York: John Wiley & Sons, 1968), chaps. 10–11.

from international competition rather than from other domestic firms, especially in sectors where considerable returns to scale have resulted in a very small number of domestic firms in a particular sector. Many systematic microeconomic case studies have also reported how firms have allowed costs per unit of output to rise when profits are high and how the rate of productivity increase has accelerated when profits have been squeezed.[30] I also believe, though this may be difficult to prove convincingly, that the relatively competitive situation in countries such as the United States and Sweden has been a strongly positive factor in promoting the high and rising efficiency in the industrial sectors of these two countries, in contrast to countries such as Great Britain, France (particularly in the past), and Czechoslovakia after World War II, and probably also a number of underdeveloped countries such as India and many Latin American countries, that adhere to more protectionist and monopolistic practices.

To summarize: From the point of view of economic efficiency, competition has a twofold role. It is because of competition (1) that prices, for factors of production as well as for commodities, are pushed down to levels where they reflect production costs ("opportunity costs"); and (2) that firms are compelled to respond to market signals. It should also be stressed, though it is self-evident, that in principle there is no necessary conflict between competition and economic planning, provided that planning relies mainly on economic incentives wthin the context of a market system, as does the "indicative planning" now emerging in Western Europe.

It is difficult to determine conclusively whether competition has fallen or risen in recent decades. Often the ten-

---

[30]See, for instance, Leibenstein.

dency to concentration within industries in many countries is taken as an indicator that competition has fallen. It is often forgotten that there are very strong forces that have worked in the other direction. The fall in transportation costs has confronted previous regional and national monopolies with national and international competition. *One* single firm in a country may be in a more competitive situation on today's international market than were five or ten national firms fifty years ago. The gradual reduction in trade restrictions and the creation of common markets have worked in the same direction. A third factor has been the enormous expansion of close substitutes for existing products, substitutes which have, in many cases, decisively increased competition for firms. A typical and classic case is that of the old monopolistic railways, which nowadays compete closely not only with the automobile and air travel but also with the telephone, telegraph, and increasingly also with television. Similar examples abound in various fields, particularly where new materials, such as plastics and artificial fibers, have been introduced.

These observations are, of course, not in conflict with the well-known attempts by individual firms to try to avoid competition as much as possible. Adam Smith emphasized the tendency of firms to collude against the interests of the consumer and concluded that a competitive economy may require strong government intervention to break up monopolies, cartels, and similar forms of collusion among firms. Entrepreneurs are often vigorous advocates of competition in all fields except their own

These arguments are of course not very important for those who reject competition between firms mainly on *moral* grounds, and they are even less impressive to those in the New Left who already regard the present level of consumption as too high. Economists, or other social scientists for that matter, have very little to say about competition versus cooperation *as a way of life*, that is, about the psychological and physical effects on the individual. Presumably, competition between *individuals*, rather than between firms, is not without its human costs, both for those who do badly and those who do well in the competitive race. For instance, in recent years there has been increasing concern in many countries (such as in Scandinavia) about human-adjustment problems connected with an accelerated rate of structural change, by itself closely related to increased international competition. However, competition among individuals presumably prevails not only in economic systems with competing firms but also in administrative hierarchies, as well as among individuals within political parties. It is also interesting to note that when people can do what they like, that is, on their leisure time, they to a very large extent go in for competitive games, such as sports or social games.

However, a society without (or with a minimum of) competition, must also face some serious problems in human relations, aside from the possibility of low efficiency and the relatively poor quality of products and services. For example, it must be difficult to find criteria other than competence (which in fact implies competition) by which to allocate manpower to different kinds of jobs, without using methods such as lotteries, arbitrary command by superior authorities, and nepotism of various kinds—phenomena which also may be frustrating for a lot of individuals. The more the class boundaries in a society are torn down and hence the more "open" the society is, the greater will be the role that will presumably fall to competition between individuals for different jobs. In a society in which everybody obtains his position by inheritance or tradition, competition for different jobs can be expected to be rather small. And, conversely, a "classless society," without discrimination based on race or family background, can be expected to be quite competitive.

THE MEANING OF "DEVELOPMENT"

Many of the previously discussed points—markets, ownership, economic incentives, competition, and centralization— were also at the center of interest for the old Left. A more original notion of the New Left is its belief that present Western capitalist societies (particularly the United States) are overdeveloped and that the level of consumption of the average citizen is already too high. It would seem that this belief is more characteristic of part of the student Left than the (somewhat older), often Marxist, authors who have inspired them.

The idea of "overconsumption" seems to have two quite different versions. One is that additional (private) consumption is, from the point of view of society as a whole, without utility or even is a source of disutility; thus, the marginal utility of consumption is in fact said to be zero, or even negative, though people have not yet discovered this for themselves. The idea is often expressed by formulations such as "it is not true that more stuff is better than less." Or, "the time of scarcity of the means of production is over."

On this point the New Left obviously deviates considerably from the old Left. One reason is presumably that the old Left basically was a workers' movement, whereas the New Left obviously is mainly a student movement. It seems that such ideas are more natural among children from middle- and high-income families still attending schools, for whom the economic problems of raising and financing a family have not yet become a reality. It is, I believe, revealing that though the student revolt in France in May

1968 was to some extent a protest against the "consumption society," when it was followed up by workers, it ended in a 13 percent wage increase designed to permit higher private consumption by wage earners (the majority of the population).

For those among the New Left who emphasize the unimportance of (additional) consumption, there may also be a problem of consistency: If (additional) consumption is so unimportant, why is *equality* in income and consumption so important?

There is, however, a second version of the "overconsumption" theory. This is the idea that private consumption is not too high by itself, but is high in relation to public consumption and to the quality of the natural and manmade environment. Thus, the marginal utility of private consumption is not assumed to be zero—only smaller than the marginal utility of public consumption and of enjoyment of the environment. Let us call this the theory of "relative" overconsumption. This is the idea that the political process has not been able to achieve optimum allocation, that is, a position in conformity with the dominating preferences in society, between private consumption, public consumption, and the quality of the environment. The "quality of life" is said to be sacrificed by too much concentration on the output of commodities and the level of private consumption, with consequent neglect of the externalities of production and consumption.[31]

Sometimes these assertions go very far. Some of those who inspire the New Left have expressed a desire for public consumption to become the "normal" way of consuming. Leo Hubernan and Paul Sweezy have declared, "We must

[31]John Kenneth Galbraith, in *The Affluent Society* (Boston: Houghton Mifflin, 1958) simultaneously embraced both these versions of the overconsumption theory, though without distinguishing between them.

build a system in which public services become the normal, indeed the *necessary* way of life and not the aberration in a few quixotic altruists."[32] It is often argued that cutting down "luxury and waste" in private consumption would make possible extraordinary achievements in public consumption. Or, as formulated by Mandel: "Abolition of luxury and waste, or obvious harmful forms of expenditure, would by itself be sufficient to make *doubling* of useful public consumption in the Western countries, that is, in particular expenditure on education, health, public transport, conservation of natural resources, etc.[33] As public consumption in these countries is usually between 10 and 20 percent of GNP and private consumption about 55 to 65 percent, a rather substantial part of private consumption must consist of "luxury and waste" (if the resources are not to be taken from defense spending, which varies between 1 and 10 percent of GNP).

Obviously, it is not necessary to assume that the marginal utility of private consumption is zero or negative or even that it is low, to argue for the allocation of more resources to public consumption and for improvement of the general environment. Moreover, maybe the charge of "overconsumption" in present-day developed economies often is simply a metaphorical way of saying that the *distribution* of income is unfair—within countries as well as between rich and poor countries. Some adherents of the New Left also seem to believe that notions of overconsumption and overdevelopment are "on their way out" of the doctrine of the movement and that stronger emphasis will instead be placed on poverty (in underdeveloped countries as well as among minority groups within developed countries).

[32]Leo Hubernan and Paul Sweezy, "Socialism Is the Only Answer," *Monthly Review* Pamphlet Series (May 1951).
[33]Mandel, 2:616.

Sometimes the allegation of overconsumption is widened to a charge that today's capitalist societies are in some sense "overdeveloped," an argument particularly often heard in the American discussion. The attempts by some New Left groups to choose "voluntary poverty" (usually for a limited period and with the possibility of returning again, at any time, to the affluent society) may serve as a symbol of these somewhat Rousseaurian ideas.

To some extent it may be a semantic question whether we prefer to call the present society of the United States over-developed or underdeveloped when we want to express personal dislike of some of its aspects. My personal pref-erences are against calling it overdeveloped, however. I would rather argue that the American society has many features characteristic of underdeveloped countries, many more in fact than some other high-income countries. To appreciate this point it should be noted that in recent years it has become more and more common to regard "develop-ment" as a *multidimensional* concept, including other di-mensions than a high average per capita income and advanced technology in the leading commodity-producing sectors, a definition according to which Kuwait and the United States would be the two most developed countries in the world. In a more multidimensional definition of development, we might also want to consider such factors as (1) the existence of inequalities (for example, large pockets of poverty and undereducation), making a country a "dual" society; (2) the disproportional political power held by certain privileged minorities, combined with dis-crimination of underprivileged minority groups; (3) the lack of security, both "elementary" personal security in the streets and social security in case of bad health or other personal misfortune; (4) the shortcomings in the quality of public services, such as schools, transportation and recreation facilities; (5) the deficiencies in the quality of the general environment, showing up in city blight and pollution; and (6) a propensity to utilize modern technology for projects that promote national prestige rather than for improvement in the living conditions of human beings—all areas in which many so-called underdeveloped countries are said to suffer. By this broader, multidimensional definition of development, it does not seem self-evident that the United States should be regarded as an "overdeveloped" country, or even a highly developed country. The rationale for claiming that the United States shows many signs of an underdeveloped country would presumably be further strengthened if we also demanded from a highly developed country a "mature" foreign policy, in the sense that relations with the outside world are handled in a nondogmatic way, with due respect for facts and for other people's right to self-determination; that is, if we required from a highly developed country that it show an ability to handle problems of "human relations" not only at home but also in the outside world.

From considerations of this sort, I find it difficult to sympathize with the belief (or, the terminology) often expressed in some New Left literature that the United States is an "overdeveloped" country. Even if it might be more appropriate to say that the United States shows considerable similarities with so-called underdeveloped countries, the clearest and simplest way to characterize the United States seems to be to point out the peculiarities in the distribution of its income and power, as well as in the allocation of its resources. However, it is also apparent that these very characteristics have been exposed to more and more intensive criticism inside the United States itself in recent years, with an increasing probability of substantial changes in the American society. It would, personally speaking, be surprising if these dramatic changes in opinions, particularly among the younger generation, do not have a dramatic impact on policies and institutions in such a free and open society as the United States.

PART THREE

WHERE DOES THE NEW LEFT ECONOMICS LEAD?

THE PRECEDING ANALYSIS should have illustrated the opening statement about the heterogeneity of the New Left movement. Its ideas cover a considerable part of the entire spectrum of political ideology, from the most individualistic to the most collectivistic, and from decentralized to centralized positions. The heterogeneity partly reflects the fact that many individuals with quite different opinions have, somewhat carelessly, been classified as "New Leftists," and partly the fact that one single individual often simultaneously holds ideas that are difficult to reconcile from a logical point of view. Of course, considerable heterogeneity can no doubt be shown to characterize other movements as well. Thus, among "conservative" political writers we find *both* adherents of the old "antiliberal" European conservative tradition, emphasizing state authority and bureaucratic stability, *and* adherents of the laissez faire tradition. And among proponents of democratic socialism we find *both* "social liberals," with strong sympathies for the mixed economy and the Welfare State, *and* believers in state control and ownership.

The main source of intellectual inspiration for the New Left has obviously been the old Left tradition, strongly influenced by Marxist ideas, though many of the opinions found in New Left literature are also strikingly similar to those in Galbraith's *The New Industrial State*—notions such as overconsumption and the artificial nature of consumer preferences; the emphasis on externalities and the quality of life; the failure to suggest a mechanism for the allocation of resources and the coordination of decisions;

the notion of an emerging symbiosis between private firms and the modern state; the stress on the increased importance of intellectuals in the production process; and the idea that the educational system is largely subordinate to the interest of the central public administration and the large corporations. Where the New Left seems to deviate most strongly from the old Left's Marxist tradition is in its sympathies for decentralization and its antipathy to bureaucracy, both in the community as a whole and in various kinds of organizations; and, further, in its interest in problems of the quality of life rather than the quantity of output, the tendency in *part* of the movement to be "anticonsumption," the stress on the role of students and intellectuals as a revolutionary vanguard; and, finally, perhaps also in a combination of a rather puritan morality in the matter of economic incentives (and consumption) with often rather nonpuritan opinions on other ethical issues.

However, I think it is safe to say that the Marxist influence in the New Left has increased in recent years (for instance, in the period 1965–1970). This even seems to hold for the United States, where the Marxist tradition in the New Left, as well as in the community as a whole, has obviously been weaker than in Europe. If this trend continues, the intellectual distance between the revolutionary old Left and the New Left may diminish substantially. In fact, many of the intellectual inspirers of the New Left are, or have been, closely connected with the revolutionary part of the old Left, particularly the Communist party. This holds not only for such "heroes" as Mao Tse-tung, Che Guevara, Ho Chi Minh, and Fidel Castro, but also for such writers as Louis Althusser, Henry Lefebvre, Ernest Mandel and Paul Baran. Moreover, the basic feature of the communist movement—the advocacy of revolution and class struggle, in contrast to the "class collaboration" preferred by the social democrats—is obviously also a salient feature of a large fraction of the New Left.

Some of the differences between the old and the New Left may be expected to remain, however, especially those related to the new world situation during the postwar period: the emergence of revolutionary movements all over the "third world"; the establishment of new communist countries such as China and Cuba, which do not accept the previously unquestioned leadership of the first socialist country, the Soviet Union; the rise of Yugoslav revisionism and the new demands in Eastern Europe for decentralization, market systems, and reliance on the profit motive and economic incentives; the criticism of the Soviet Union by communist revolutionaries beyond the reach of Soviet power, such as Che Guevara and Mao Tse-tung; the Sino-Soviet split; the consolidation of a rigid bureaucratic system in the Soviet Union; the tendencies pointing to a permanent *pax Sovietico-Americana;* and the emergence of capitalist societies characterized by a wide range of opportunities for employment, general affluence, and a Welfare State, rather than unemployment and mass poverty.

All these events make it difficult to create a unified communist movement such as that which emerged during the period between the two world wars. For this reason it seems realistic to expect that in the future the New Left will also be much more heterogeneous than the old communist Left.

Depending on the particular aspect of the New Left's beliefs and ideas that is stressed, adherents will wind up in rather different political stables. A schematic classification of these may clarify the issue.

Anarchism. If the refusal to accept organized authority

is emphasized, the anarchistic solution is obviously chosen, as has been the case with various radical student leaders (for example, Cohn-Bendit). The anarchist position is probably most useful in the world of art, where the economic problems of the world are "solved" by symbolic acts, for instance, the burning of money on the stage by the Living Theatre. An anarchistic organization of the economy is, for obvious reasons, difficult to conceive, as soon as we discuss economies that are not the isolated small enclaves of the Robinson-Crusoe type (for which, incidentally, economic theory has been rather well developed, as a pedagogical device in older economics textbooks).

Laissez faire. If a market system is added to the anarchistic model, we are in the world of laissez faire economics. For such an economy a very well-developed economic theory undoubtedly exists. The practical consequence of this position would presumably be the desire to do away with government regulations, to improve competition by subdividing existing firms, and to cut down drastically the ambitions of economic policy and the activities of the Welfare State. In a New Left version of laissez faire, we should probably assume that the firms are owned and operated on some kind of cooperative basis (a system of producers' cooperatives or collective capitalism) or possibly some other kind of public ownership and control.

I do not think that the loss in economic efficiency connected with returns to scale would be dramatic if big American companies were subdivided, for instance, five or even ten times. The average cost curve seems to be rather flat over long intervals, and the experience of relatively small firms (internationally speaking), like manufacturing firms in Sweden, for instance, do not indicate that firms have to be nearly as large as those in the United States to be efficient, particularly as an increase in competition by itself is likely to increase efficiency.

For small countries, the possibility of dividing existing firms into several independent units without considerable loss in efficiency is of course more limited. In fact, it would seem that considerable returns to scale could be reaped in certain sectors of the raw-material refining industries (pulp, paper, iron, and steel) in the small European countries by agglomeration of firms into fewer and larger units. For such countries, competition and a reduction in the market power of large corporations have to be obtained by free trade and common markets.

The important objection to the laissez faire solution is, in my opinion, that we would then have to accept the well-known "market failures," such as economic instability; an unequal distribution of income; external effects which are not automatically taken care of; and various types of insecurity for the individual which private insurance systems will not do away with. If the activities of public authorities are strongly curtailed, there is also a possibility that collective consumption will not be well looked after.

The liberal–social democratic solution. If the public authorities are anxious to fight "market failures"—instability, inequality, externalities, deficiencies of collective consumption—we wind up in the liberal–social democratic Welfare State, with stabilization policy, redistribution policy, intervention to handle external effects, antimonopoly policy, strong attempts to provide collective services and the like. Some public enterprises may be used in carrying out this solution—to improve competition, to regulate natural monopolies, to help redistribute wealth, and to increase the area of parliamentary control of the economy. The ambitions of economic planning, the energy devoted to the achievement of equality, and possibly the degree of nationalization, may serve to differentiate between the liberal and social democratic versions of the Welfare State.

As a matter of fact, the first political program of the

American SDS movement (the Port Huron statement in 1962) can best be characterized as a liberal–social democratic program. Not until later did the movement develop in the direction of Marxism, communism, anarchism, Trotskyism, and Maoism. Other factions in the New Left have all the time been quite critical of the liberal–social democratic Welfare State, with a "mixed economy."

Market socialism. If there is substantial nationalization in the social democratic Welfare State, so that the public sector dominates the economy, we wind up in the world of market socialism, toward which some Eastern European countries *may* gradually be moving, though still without the democratic institutions characteristic of the liberal–social democratic model. The characteristics of this model resemble those of the liberal–social democratic one, except for the structure of ownership (and, possibly, the political system). A characteristic feature of this model is that inequalities in the distribution of *capital* and *capital incomes* can be minimized—in the case of physical and financial capital. As we have seen, however, some problems of this model cannot easily be solved—among them the distribution of power, the choice of goals by individual firms, and the stimulation of *new* initiative by persons other than those who have already reached the top of established hierarchies. In general, it seems that the model of market socialism has not attracted wide interest, and probably not wide sympathy either, in New Left literature.

Nonmarket system with collective ownership. Because of their aversion to markets, competition, and economic incentives, many New Left adherents do not seem willing to accept any of the preceding models. Even though many of them also dislike bureaucracy, nevertheless, they would have to accept administratively run economic systems which, to arrive at consistent decisions, must be coordinated by central authorities. Then we come close to the traditional Soviet model, which seems to have some advocates in the New Left movement, among them Baran and Sweezy, though they all object to specific features of the Soviet bureaucracy, often without realizing that bureaucracy is a necessary part of the model.

Despite its criticism of the Soviet dictatorship and demands for more democratic institutions, the New Left can hardly be said typically to argue for a transformation of society into democratic and parliamentary forms. Instead, the need for revolutionary action by nonparliamentary methods is stressed in much New Left literature. The "dictatorship of the proletariat," for some unspecified time; revolutionary "direct" action against factories, universities, and other institutions; and the seizure of power by physical force, seem to be essential parts of most New Left positions. There are probably also advocates of democratic procedures in the movement, determined to "vote" the community into socialism; this stand does not seem to be typical of the New Left movement, however.

This is not the place for a detailed account of the advantages and disadvantages of armed revolution in various types of society. It is, of course, quite possible than an economic, social, and possibly also (in the long run) democratic development sometimes may be speeded up by armed revolt—in less romantic terms, by "civil war." In fact, this method may in some cases be the *only* conceivable way (within the foreseeable future). One problem, though, is that the human sufferings (unknown in advance) during and immediately after a revolution might not be fully compensated by the gains which may be achieved by the revolt. Personally, I have also always been surprised by the fact that the very same individuals who are against the idea that conflicts *between* countries should be solved by military force, often and perhaps even without much reservation regard armed force as a necessary and suitable method for solving problems and conflicts *within* countries. There does not seem to be much evidence that civil wars are less brutal than wars between countries. Skeptics about the advantages of civil war—a group for which I feel strong sympathy—can also point to the risk that the selection of political leaders through competition in physical violence may not be very "good." Is it not rather likely that leaders emerging as a result of this type of selection process may often be both authoritarian and cruel? The possibility that revolution, in fact, only means a substitution of oppressors hardly lacks historical illustrations.

Thus, depending on which particular aspect of the New Left's arguments is emphasized—criticism of authority, refusal to accept market systems, sympathy either for decentralization or for central planning, awareness of the market failures in the laissez faire model, refusal to accept democratic rules to transform society—quite different political "stables," or parties, may be discovered within New Left ideology. In fact, the New Left is an example of a political movement covering a substantial part of the spectrum of socioeconomic and political ideas.

What a social scientist perhaps misses most of all in New Left literature and its discussions is an awareness of the enormous difficulties involved in solving the problems which arise in *any* social and economic system. There is a general tendency among the New Left to argue as if all, or most, difficulties could be removed "in one shot" by "revolution" or by "collective" ownership or both. As all serious scholars know, the real problems start *after* the revolution or, what from this point of view is about the same thing, *without* a revolution. However, there is very little, if any, discussion in the literature of the New Left about the *methods* of solving the problems which chiefly worry economists, such as the reconciliation of full employment with price stability and equilibrium in the balance of payments; the determination of an optimal growth rate and hence an optimal combination of consumption today and consumption tomorrow, and the manner in which this optimum is to be achieved; the design of a workable compromise between the income differentials needed to give incentives for work and for the allocation of the labor force, and the desire for equality; whether the government should intervene against "persuasive" advertising for commodities; the determination of the demand curves for public goods and services if these are not supplied on a market; whether employees in the public sector should have the right to strike; what the best combination of regulations and tax-subsidy programs is with which to cope with external effects on our environment; how to avoid an enormous concentration of power in a small group of politicians and administrators in a society with growing government intervention; what the best combination of competition and planning is in various sectors of the economy; what effects different market forms have on economic efficiency and the process of innovation; whether a decentralization of initiatives and individual freedom can be preserved in an economy with collective ownership; the advantages and disadvantages of multinational firms; whether important decisions of social and economic policy can really be efficiently carried out by the national state (such as decisions on monetary policy, environmental disruption, and taxation of multinational firms); and the like. On most of these difficult and important problems the New Left is quite silent or superficial.

What, then, are the merits of the New Left's writings? Perhaps we can say that the main contribution of the New

Left has been to remind us once more of a number of eternal problems in the political debate—issues of ownership, distribution of income and power, externalities, public participation, and social values in general—aspects which have sometimes tended to disappear from the political debate during the postwar period, perhaps especially in the United States. In this way the New Left has presumably helped to increase interest in issues of principle and ideology and perhaps also the sense of social responsibility in political debate—even though the questions New Left raises often seem to be more interesting than its answers.

•